Discover **Bruges**

The highlights of Bruges

The 10 classic places that no one should miss!

1

Rozenhoedkaai and the Bruges canals, a typical city view

The Rozenhoedkaai (Rosary Quay) links the Belfry with the city's network of canals, the true 'veins' of Bruges, and offers a unique and picturesque panoramic view. Hardly surprising, then, that the Rozenhoedkaai is the most popular photographic hotspot in town! You can discover many more special places and hidden gems during a boat trip on the canals. From the water, Bruges is even more enchanting. A classic that you really don't want to miss.

Markt, an absolute must

2

The vibrant centre of the city has been dominated for centuries by the 83-metre high Belfry. Today, you can climb right to the top of this impressive tower. You will be rewarded with a spectacular view of Bruges and the surrounding countryside. The Markt (Market Square) is also home to the Historium, a top attraction that takes you back in time to the city's medieval past. Surrounded by colourful houses, the Market Square is also the regular standing place for the famous horse-drawn carriages.

(Read more on pages 56 and 65.)

Medieval splendour on the Burg

The Burg is the beating heart of the city. From the 14th century town hall, which is the oldest in the Low Countries, Bruges has been governed for more than 600 years. This majestic architectural square also contains the Palace of the Liberty of Bruges, the former Civil Registry and the Basilica of the Holy Blood. No other location in Bruges bears greater testimony to the city's former wealth. *(Read more on pages 55, 59 and 73.)*

Strolling through the old Hansa Quarter

From the 13th to the 15th century, Bruges was the most important trading centre in northwestern Europe. Spanish merchants settled along the Spaanse Loskaai (Spanish Quay) and in the Spanjaardstraat. The Germans or Easterners – 'oosterlingen' in Dutch – took up residence in the Oosterlingenplein. In this old Hansa Quarter, you can admire the mansions of the wealthy international merchants and the great trading nations of the day. You can almost still smell the atmosphere of the Middle Ages.

The Flemish primitives: timeless beauty

In Bruges' golden century – the 15th century – art was a big deal. Leading artists of the day, like Jan van Eyck and Hans Memling, came to live and work in the city. Today, you can marvel at the masterpieces of the world-famous Flemish primitives in the Groeninge Museum and the St. John's Hospital. And in the treasury of Bruges' oldest parish church, Saint Saviour's Cathedral, you can also come face to face with other priceless paintings that were created in the city in centuries gone by.
(Read more on pages 63-64 and 70-72.)

Burgundian splendour

Discover Burgundian splendour at the renovated site of the Gruuthuse Museum, a luxurious 15th century city palace that will reopen its doors in 2019. The museum's rich collection will guide you through 500 years of Bruges history. An intimate prayer chapel links the palace with the adjacent Church of Our Lady. In this way, the lords of Gruuthuse were able to follow the religious services in comfort and privacy. The church's showpiece is the beautiful white marble statue of the *Madonna and Child* by Michelangelo, which leaves no visitor unmoved.
(Read more on pages 53, 64 and 67.)

Quiet contemplation in the Beguinage

Some places are so beautiful that they leave you speechless. The Beguinage is just such a place. This is where the beguines – emancipated women who lived pious and chaste lives without taking holy orders – once lived together in harmony. This walled oasis of religious peace, with its delightful inner garden, wind-twisted trees and white-painted gables, can charm even the most cynical of souls with its deafening silence.
(Read more on pages 55-56.)

Minnewater: romance all the way

This small rectangular lake was once the mooring place for the barges that sailed the inland waterways between Bruges and Ghent. Nowadays, together with the Minnewater Park, this stretch of water – whose name means 'Lake of love' – is the most romantic spot in the city. The Minnewater Bridge offers magical views over one of the most idyllic places in Bruges.

Concert Hall, or Culture with a capital C

This tall and stately culture temple on 't Zand gives the largest square of Bruges its own unique dynamism. In the soberly decorated auditorium, visitors can enjoy classical music and contemporary dance in the best possible setting. During the day, you can explore this remarkable building by following the Concertgebouw Circuit, an original and entertaining experience route that ends with a fantastic view of Bruges from the roof terrace. *(Read more on pages 60, 77 and 84.)*

Almshouses: charity embodied in stone

Villages within the city. That's how you can best describe these residential centres, which originated in medieval times and are still occupied today by senior citizens. The almshouses were first founded centuries ago for charitable purposes. Today, with their picturesque gardens, their white-painted gables and their perfect peace and quiet, they are amongst the most tranquil places in Bruges. *(Read more on page 14.)*

Walk 1

Bruges, proud world heritage city

Bonifaciusbrug

Bruges may be, quite rightly, very proud of her world heritage status, but the city is happily embracing the future too! This walk takes you along world-famous panoramic views, sky-high monuments and centuries-old squares invigorated by contemporary constructions. One foot planted in the Middle Ages, the other one firmly planted in the present. This walk is an absolute must for first-time visitors who would like to explore the very heart of the city straight away. Keep your camera at the ready!

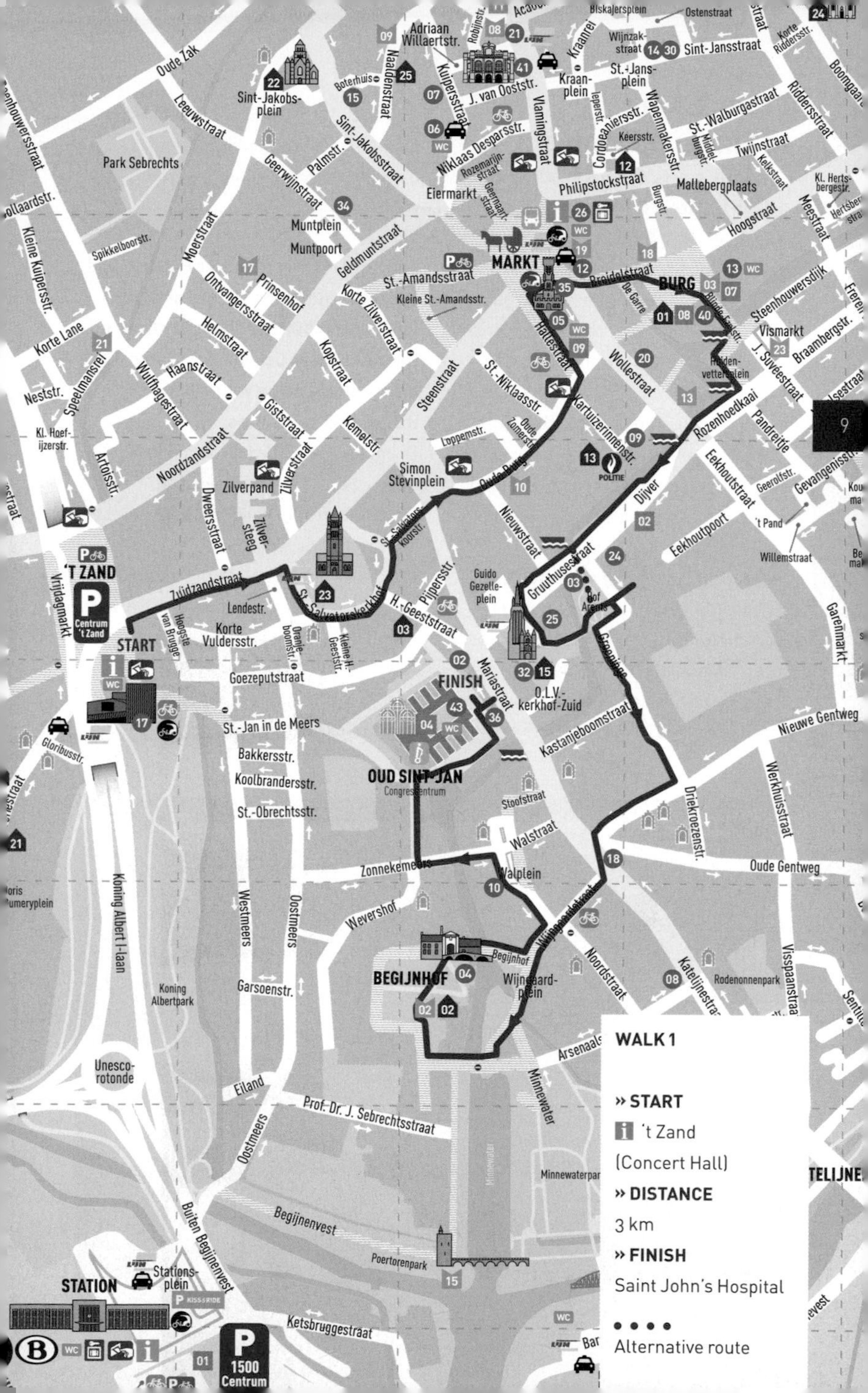

WALK 1

» START

't Zand

(Concert Hall)

» DISTANCE

3 km

» FINISH

Saint John's Hospital

• • • •
Alternative route

From 't Zand to Simon Stevinplein

This walk starts at the i tourist office 't Zand (Concert Hall).

't Zand, Bruges' largest square, is dominated by the Concert Hall 17, one of Bruges' most talked-about buildings. Clear-cut proof that this world heritage city isn't afraid of the future. The Concertgebouw Circuit 17 will take you behind the scenes and right to the very top of this magnificent building, where you can find an interactive space for sound art. You can also enjoy the wonderful view over the Bruges skyline. Don't forget to drop in at the i tourist office 't Zand (Concert Hall) on the ground floor: here you will find all the necessary tourist information as well as expert advice on all cultural events, and you can buy your tickets immediately.

On pages 112-115, you can learn more about the Concert Hall and the Concertgebouw Circuit in an interview with Ayako Ito.

Leave i 't Zand (Concert Hall) behind you, walk along the square and turn into Zuidzandstraat, the first street on the right. Saint Saviour's Cathedral 23 looms up ahead on your right after three hundred metres.

Bruges' oldest parish church is located on a lower level than the present Zuidzandstraat, which is situated on an old sand ridge. What's more, in the Middle Ages people simply threw their refuse out onto the street where it was then flattened by passing carts and coaches. This raised the street level even further. Inside Saint Saviour's, the church tower's wooden rafters can be

23

BURG SQUARE: AN ARCHITECTURAL SYNOPSIS

Art lovers have already noticed that the Burg projects a wonderful cross-section of stunning architectural styles. It is, indeed, a summary of all the styles that have caught our imagination throughout the centuries in one place. From Romanesque (Saint Basil's Church) and Gothic (City Hall) by way of Renaissance (Civil Registry) and Baroque (Deanery) to Classicism (Mansion of the Liberty of Bruges). There's no need to go and dash all around Bruges to see it all!

lit. The cathedral treasury displays interesting copper memorial plaques, fine examples of gold and silver and paintings by Dieric Bouts, Hugo van der Goes and Pieter Pourbus.

Turn right before the cathedral into Sint-Salvatorskerkhof. Walk around the cathedral and take the fourth street on the right, the Sint-Salvatorskoorstraat. This will take you to the Simon Stevinplein.

This attractive square, lined with cosy restaurant terraces in summertime, is named after Simon Stevin, a well-known Flemish-Dutch scientist. His gracious statue naturally takes centre stage.

Markt and Burg

Continue down Oude Burg, a street in the right-hand corner of the square. Before long, you will see the Cloth Halls 09 on your left. These belong to the Belfry 05. You're allowed to cross the halls' imposing inner courtyard between 8.00 a.m. and 6.00 p.m. during the week, and between 9.00 a.m. and 6.00 p.m. on Saturday. Markt is at the other end of the courtyard. If the gate is closed, turn back and walk down Hallestraat, which runs parallel to the Halls.

Walk 2 (see pages 24-25) comments more extensively on Markt.

Return to the Belfry 05 and walk down Breidelstraat, a traffic-free alley on the corner to the left. Continue to the Burg square.

03 07

Along the road to your right you will notice De Garre, a narrow alley. While this may be the narrowest street in Bruges (try walking side by side here!), it nevertheless boasts a fair number of cosy cafés. The Burg is the most majestic square in the city, so take your time to admire its grandeur. The main character in this medieval story is the City Hall 08 40 (1376-1420), one of the oldest city halls in the Netherlands and a Gothic example for all its brothers and sisters that were built later, from Louvain to Audenarde and Brussels. Having admired its exterior, enter the impressive Gothic Hall and gaze in admiration at the polychrome floating ribs of the vaulted ceiling. Hiding on the right-hand side of this Gothic monument is the Basilica of the Holy Blood 01. It was originally dedicated to both Our Lady and Saint Basil, and was built as a fortress church on two levels between 1139 and 1157.

The lower church has retained its Romanesque character. The upper chapel, which was originally little more than a kind of balcony, was gradually extended over the years to become a church in its own right. It was only during the 19th century that it was renovated in the neo-Gothic style that can be seen today. The sacred relic of the Holy Blood has been kept here since the 13th century. In a tradition dating back to at least 1304, each year on Ascension Day the relic is carried in the Holy Blood Procession, a popular event that captures the imagination of the entire city and which in 2009 was classified by UNESCO as part of the world's Intangible Cultural Heritage. Facing the basilica is the gleaming Renaissance façade of the old Civil Registry 03 (1534-1537, which now houses the City Archive 07 adjacent to the Liberty of Bruges 13.

Its showpiece is a splendid oak mantelpiece with an alabaster frieze (1529). From the adjoining Palace of the Liberty of Bruges (the front part of which dates from 1722), the countryside in a wide area around the city was once governed. After 1795, the building became a courtroom and since 1988 it has housed various branches of the city administration. Once upon a time, the impressive Saint Donatian's Cathedral graced the spot directly in front of the City Hall. The church was torn down in 1799 during the French occupation. The adjacent Dean-

23

ery 18 (1655-1666), which still stands, was once the seat of the dean or spiritual leader of Saint Donation's. For those who are interested: in the Crowne Plaza Hotel's cellar, you can visit the foundations of a part of Saint Donatian's Cathedral (free of charge).

Fishy stories

Proceed to Blinde-Ezelstraat, the little street to the left of the City Hall. Don't forget to look back at the lovely arch between the City Hall and the Old Civil Registry 03 07. Do you see Solomon? Left of him is the statue of Prosperity, to the right the statue of Peace.

According to tradition, Blinde-Ezelstraat (Blind Donkey Street) owes its name to a tavern of the same name. In olden days, the breweries that delivered beer to the taverns in the city used donkeys to turn their treadmills. To stop the poor beasts from realizing that they were just going around in circles, they were fitted with a blindfold. From the bridge, a few metres further along on the left, you can see the Meebrug (1390), one of the oldest bridges in the city.

Vismarkt 23 opens up immediately past the bridge.

Originally, fish was sold on the corner of the main market square, where the Historium 26 now stands, but the fish sellers were forced to move here in the 18th century because of the smell. In the covered arcade, specially constructed for the purpose in 1821, fresh seafood was sold, a delicacy that only the rich could afford. Today you can still buy your fresh saltwater fish here every morning from Wednesday to Saturday. In the summer, the Vismarkt is a fun spot for regular dance and music events, where you can also get a bite to eat and something to drink.

Meebrug

Retrace your steps and turn left in front of the bridge towards Huidenvettersplein.
Whereas Vismarkt served the rich, Huidenvettersplein (Tanners Square) served the poor. No sea fish on the menu here, but affordable freshwater fish. The post in the middle of the square used to have a twin brother: between the two posts hung the scales that the fish were weighed on. The large, striking building dominating the square used to be the meeting hall of the tanners. Here they sold the cow hides that they had turned into leather. The location was not chosen by chance: tanning leather was a smelly business and because the wind mainly came from the north or north-west, the foul smells were blown away from the city, towards fields that were then unoc-

ALMSHOUSES, THE QUICKEST WAY TO HEAVEN

These charitable dwellings were built from the 14th century onwards. Sometimes by the trade guilds, who wanted to offer their ageing members a roof over their heads; sometimes by widows or wealthy citizens, who hoped to secure their place in heaven with a display of Christian charity. To stake their claim, each residential centre had its own chapel, where the residents offered prayers of thanks to God, as the household rules prescribed. Practically all of the almshouses have been carefully restored and modernised and offer cosy living to today's elderly, whilst their small yet picturesque gardens and white-painted façades offer welcoming peace and quiet to the present-day visitor. Feel free to enter these premises, but don't forget to respect their perfect tranquillity.
(On the City map the almshouses are indicated by ⌂ .)

cupied. So the statue on the corner of the building has good reason to turn his nose up...

Continue to Rozenhoedkaai. Keep right.
Rozenhoedkaai is the most photographed spot in Bruges. So, take out your camera! This was once the place where the salt traders loaded and unloaded their goods. Salt was the gold of the Middle Ages: you could use it both to preserve food and to give added flavour to your cooking. Its value is underlined by the fact that the origin of the modern word *salary* comes from the Latin word *sal*, which means 'salt'. Roman soldiers used to be paid in salt.

From Groeninge to the Bonifacius Bridge

Continue along Dijver.
Along this atmospheric stretch of water, you will first find the College of Europe (numbers 9 to 11) 02, an international postgraduate institution that focuses on European affairs, and then the Groeninge Museum (number 12) 24, Bruges' most renowned museum. On display are world-famous masterpieces by Jan van Eyck, Hans Memling, Hugo van der Goes, Gerard David and many other Flemish primitives. The museum also has a valuable collection of Flemish expressionists, neoclassical top-notch paintings from the 18th and 19th centuries and post-war modern art. Overall, the museum shows a complete overview of Belgian and southern Dutch painting from the 15th to the 20th century. The museum entrance is reached through a few picturesque courtyard gardens.
Would you like to find out more about the Flemish primitives? Then leaf through to the interview on pages 104-107 with Till-Holger Borchert, the Groeninge Museum's chief curator.

Continue along Dijver. The entrance gate to the Gruuthuse Museum 25 is on your left, just beyond the little bridge.
This museum reopens its doors in spring after a long period of renovation.
You can read more about the Gruuthuse Museum in Walk 2 (on pages 22-23) and on page 53.

Continue to Guido Gezelleplein, then turn left in front of the Church of Our Lady 15 32 and follow the narrow footpath to the picturesque Bonifacius Bridge. Due to renovation works (until spring 2019), it is possible that the foot-

25

path will be closed for a time. If this is the case, follow the alternative route as indicated on the map (dotted line).
The crosses that you see all over the place don't belong to graves at all – they are crosses taken down from church steeples during the First World War to disorientate the enemy spies. The crosses have never been put up again. Close to the Bonifacius Bridge is Bruges' smallest Gothic window. Look up! It was through this window that the lords and ladies of Gruuthuse were able to peer down onto their private jetty. Across the bridge is the charming city garden Hof Arents of the Arentshuis (16th-19th century) 03, an elegant 17th-century abode. The top floor houses work by the versatile British artist Frank Brangwyn. The ground floor is reserved for temporary exhibitions. The most striking features in the garden are the last two remaining columns of the Water Halls, the central storage depot for shipping that once stood on the Market Square, and the group of statues by Rik Poot (1924-2006) depicting *The Four Horsemen of the Apocalypse*: pestilence, war, famine and death. The religious theme of Rik Poots' group of statues also appealed centuries earlier to the artist Hans Memling, since the horsemen are also present in his *St. John Triptych*, which can be seen in the nearby St. John's Hospital 36. The garden gate leads through to the Groeninge Museum 24, where you can admire more works by Memling and his contemporaries.

On to the Beguinage!

Leave the museum garden of the Groeninge Museum through the narrow garden gate and turn left into Groeninge, a winding street. Turn right at the intersection with Nieuwe Gentweg.

02 02

Minnewater

Pop into the Saint Joseph and the De Meulenaere almshouses (both from the 17th century). Then continue down the street.

On the left-hand corner of Oude Gentweg and Katelijnestraat is the Diamond Museum 18, Bruges' most glittering museum and the place to be for all lovers of bling. It goes without saying that an inspiring diamond museum simply couldn't be absent in the most romantic city of the western hemisphere!

Turn left into Katelijnestraat, then immediately right into Wijngaardstraat. Cross Wijngaardplein – a stopping place for coachmen. A little further on, turn right onto the bridge beside the Sashuis (lock house) to enter the Beguinage. The bridge offers a fine view of the Minnewater.

The Minnewater used to be the landing stage of the barges or track boats that provided a regular connection between Bruges and Ghent. Today it is one of Bruges' most romantic beauty spots.

Equally atmospheric, yet of a totally different nature, is the Beguinage. Although the 'Princely Beguinage Ten Wijngaarde' 02 02, founded in 1245, is no longer occupied by beguines (devout and celibate women who formed a religious community without taking holy orders), but by a number of nuns of the Order of St. Benedict and unmarried Bruges women, you can still form an excellent picture of what daily life looked like in the 17th century at the Beguine's house 04. The imposing courtyard garden, the white-painted house fronts and blessed peace create an atmosphere all of its own. The entrance gates are closed each day at 6.30 p.m. without fail.

Walk around the Beguinage and leave through the main gate. Turn left after the bridge and left again to reach Walplein.

De Halve Maan 10, a brewery established as early as 1564, is at number 26 (on your left-hand side). This is Bruges'

Walplein

oldest active city brewery. Their speciality is *Brugse Zot* (Bruges' Fool), a spirited top-fermented beer made from malt, hop and special yeast. The name of the beer refers to the nickname of the Bruges townspeople, a name allegedly conferred upon them by Maximilian of Austria. In order to welcome the duke, the citizens paraded past him in a lavish procession of brightly coloured merrymakers and fools. When a short time later they asked their ruler to finance a new 'zothuis', or madhouse, his answer was as short as it was forceful: *'The only people I have seen here are fools. Bruges is one big madhouse. Just close the gates.'*

A splendid finish at Saint John's Hospital

Turn left into Zonnekemeers. Once across the water, enter the Oud Sint-Jan (Old St. John) site on the right. Feel free to walk through the 19th century carriage house, if the gate is open.

The former St. John's Hospital (12th-19th century) 36 which you can see in the right-hand corner, boasts a history stretching back more than 800 years. The oldest documents date from the year 1188! It was here that monks and

TIP

At the heart of the Old Saint John site, you will discover the 19th century infirmary wards of Saint John's Hospital. Make sure you go inside. On some days, you might catch a free concert by the Bruges harpist Luc Vanlaere and be moved by his wonderful sounds. In addition, the historic infirmary wards are frequently the setting for temporary expositions by Xpo Center Bruges. So why not take a moment to see what's on during your visit to Bruges? *For more info, see www.harpmuziek.be and www.xpo-center-bruges.be.*

nuns cared for pilgrims, travellers, the poor and the sick. Often, they came to the hospital to die. According to tradition, the painter Hans Memling was once a patient. After he was cured, he rewarded those who had treated him with four paintings. In the 19th century, two other Memling paintings found their way to the hospital, so that six of his masterpieces can now be admired here. Immediately in front of the convent of the old hospital stands the sculpture *The Veins of the Convent*, a work by the contemporary Italian artist Giuseppe Penone, which refers in a symbolic way to both the monastic way of life and the care function with which this site was once so closely associated. *Read more about Italian art in Bruges in the interview with Sonia Papili on pages 96-99.* Or how history still feeds the present – what could be more appropriate for a world heritage city like Bruges!

Turn left at the corner and then go right immediately.

In the open space of the courtyard you will find the herb garden and the entrance to the 17th century pharmacy, which is well worth a visit. In the garden, you can see many of the plants that are listed in an 18th century recipe book, which is on display in the pharmacy. Retrace your steps, turn left and walk through the passage. The entrance to the imposing medieval hospital wards, its church and chapel, the Diksmuide attic and the old dormitory are just around the corner to the right.

Carriage house

Walk 2

Bruges, a Burgundian city

Ceremonial tomb of Mary of Burgundy, Church of Our Lady

When Philip the Bold, Duke of Burgundy, married Margaret of Dampierre, the daughter of the last Count of Flanders, in the 14th century, the county of Flanders suddenly found itself belonging to Burgundy. As the Burgundian court liked to stay in Bruges, the port city became a magnet for noblemen, merchants and artists. They naturally all wanted to get their share of the city's wealth. Today the Burgundian influence is still strongly felt throughout Bruges. Let's discover a northern city with a southern character.

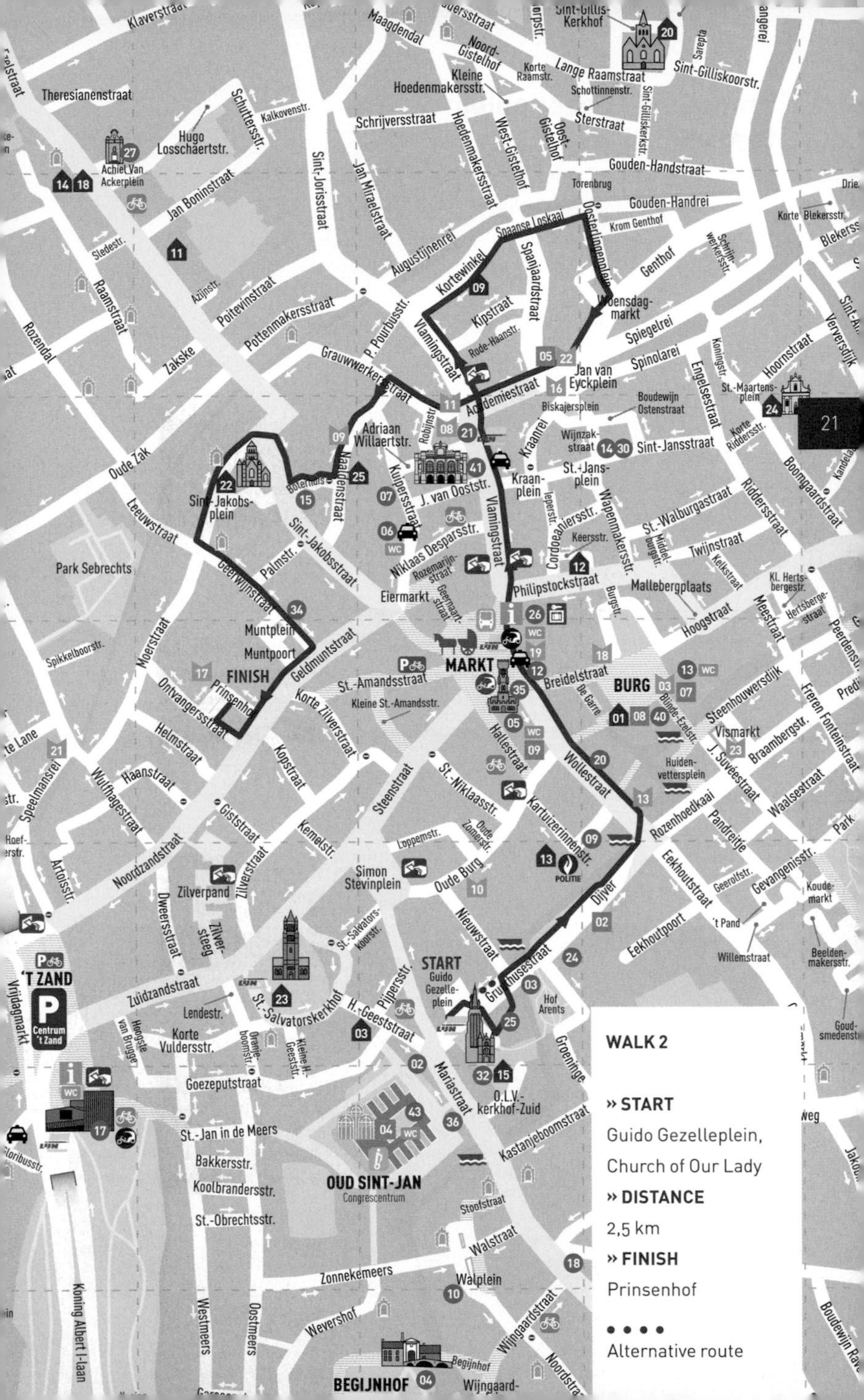

WALK 2

» START

Guido Gezelleplein, Church of Our Lady

» DISTANCE

2,5 km

» FINISH

Prinsenhof

• • • • Alternative route

From Guido Gezelleplein to Markt

This square is named after the Flemish priest and poet Guido Gezelle (1830-1899). Take a seat on one of the square's benches and enjoy Gezelle's lovely statue and the side-view of the Church of Our Lady 15 32. Its one hundred and fifteen (and a half!)-metre high brick tower is sure proof of the craftsmanship of Bruges' builders. Marvel at the rich art collection inside, from Michelangelo's world-famous *Madonna and Child* to the 15th and 16th century tombs of Mary of Burgundy and Charles the Bold. On your left is the striking residence of the lords of Gruuthuse, now the Gruuthuse Museum 25, which reopens its doors in spring after a long period of interior and exterior renovation works. The well (which unfortunately cannot be seen from the Guido Gezelleplein) and the tower were status symbols, and evidence of the Gruuthuse family's great wealth. They made their fortune from their exclusive rights to 'gruut', a herb mixture that, ages before hop, was used to flavour beer. Louis of Gruuthuse not only commanded the army of Duke Charles the Bold, he was also the personal bodyguard to his daughter Mary of Burgundy. In addition, he was a patron of the arts and the owner of the famous Gruuthuse manuscript that bears his name, a famous medieval collection of no fewer than 147 songs (amongst other things). His family motto *'Plus est en*

DID YOU KNOW?

For more than ten years, the towers of the Church of Our Lady and St. Saviour's Cathedral have been the preferred nesting locations for a pair of peregrine falcons. These lightning-fast birds of prey are welcome guests because they are the ideal weapon in the never-ending fight against the nuisance caused by... pigeons.

25

TIP

During the 16th century, the impressive mansion on the corner of the Wollestraat was once the home of Juan Perez de Malvenda, son of the Consul of the Spanish Nation and one of the city's most important residents. For a time, he kept the relic of the Holy Blood here. On the ground floor you can find a collection of all the things for which Belgium is famous: from a limitless choice of regional beers, through delicious biscuits and traditionally made jams, to fantastic old-fashioned sweets. The well-hidden terrace offers a magnificent view over the Rosary Quay.

vous' stands proudly above the door of the residence. Today, this translates as: 'There is more in you (than you think)'. *(Read more about the renovated Gruuthuse Musem on pages 53 and 64.)*

Continue along the narrow footpath to the left of the church. Due to renovation works (until spring 2019), it is possible that this footpath will not be accessible.
Look up immediately beyond the bend. Do you see the chapel that seems to hold the Gruuthuse Museum and the Church of Our Lady in a close embrace? As the lords of Gruuthuse were far too grand to mingle with the populace, they had their own private chapel high above the street, where they could follow Mass.

Retrace your steps and enter the beautiful Gruuthuse courtyard (as from this spring, you can walk through the new glass reception pavilion). If you cross the square, you will pass the well. Leave the courtyard through the gate and turn right into Dijver.
Number 12 is the Groeninge Museum 24, Bruges' most famous museum. *An interview with chief curator Till-Holger Borchert is on pages 104-107.* Further along Dijver is one of the locations of the College of Europe 02, numbers 9-11, an international postgraduate institution that focuses on Europe.

Carry on down Dijver and turn left into Wollestraat.
Perez de Malvenda 13 is an impressive mansion on the corner of Wollestraat. This building, originally a mansion dating from the 13th century, has been restored from top to bottom and now houses a food store. Just before the Markt are the Cloth Halls 09, the Belfry's 05 warehouses and sales outlets. There were numerous stables with all sorts of herbs for medicinal purpose and potions along the street side until long after the Burgundian period. Indeed, Bruges being an important trading centre could by then import and sell a variety of herbs from all over Europe.

Markt, Bruges' beating heart

Wollestraat leads to Markt.

THE RIGHT TIME

Markt

On the Markt, at the very top of the late-Gothic corner house 'Bouchoute', which is currently home to the Meridian 3 tearoom, there is a shining ball decorated with gold leaf. At the time of the inauguration of the Brussels-Ghent-Bruges railway line, people were aware that the clocks in Belgium did not all keep the same time. This problem was solved by Professor Quetelet, who installed meridian lines and noonday markers in various cities, which would show precisely in each case when it was 12 o'clock midday. This was done in Bruges in 1837. This meridian ran diagonally over the Markt and is now marked by a series of copper nails. When the shadow of the golden ball falls on the meridian, it is midday precisely: 12.00 p.m. local solar time.

The Market Square (Markt) is dominated by its Belfry 05, for centuries the city's foremost edifice and the perfect lookout in case of war, fire or any other calamity. You can still climb to the top of the tower, but you will need to conquer no fewer than 366 steps to get there! Fortunately, there are a couple of places during your ascent where you can stop for a breather. Once at the top, you will be rewarded with an unforgettable panoramic view. Roughly in the middle of the square stand the statues of Jan Breydel and Pieter de Coninck, two Bruges heroes,

TIP

As you are climbing your way to the top of the Belfry tower, why not stop for a break at the vaulted treasure chamber, where the city's charters, seal and public funds were all kept during medieval times. You can make a second stop at the 'Stenen Vloer' (Stone Floor): here you will learn everything you ever wanted to know about the clock, the drum and the carillon of 47 harmonious bells, which together weigh a staggering 27 tons of pure bronze. With a little bit of luck you will be able to see the bell-ringer right at the very top, playing the keyboard with his fist, just a few steps below the bells themselves. *Each week there are free carillon concerts.* *You can read more about this on page 83.*

who since the publication of the historical novel *De Leeuw van Vlaanderen* (The Lion of Flanders) in the 19th century have enjoyed great popular acclaim because of their role in the Battle of the Golden Spurs (Flemish resistance against French rule in 1302). Their statue neatly looks out onto the Gothic revival style Provincial Court (Markt 3) 19. Until the end of the 18th century, this side of the Markt was dominated by the Water Halls (Waterhalle), a large covered area where ships moored to be loaded and unloaded, right in the very heart of the city. In medieval times, the canals ran through and across the square, as indeed they still do, although they are now in underground tunnels. Do you feel like taking a relaxing break from all that walking? Then why not treat yourself to a coach ride and explore the city for half an hour from the luxury of a horse-drawn carriage *(see page 47)* or for 30 minutes from the back of a man-powered bike carriage *(see page 50)*? If neither of these is really your thing, you can always take the classic 50-minute City Tour by minibus *(see page 48)*. Afterwards, you can simply resume your walk where you left off.

From Markt to Jan van Eyckplein

Keep Markt on your left and continue straight ahead to Vlamingstraat.

Since the 13th century, this used to be the harbour area's shopping street. A fair number of banks had a branch here, and wine taverns were two a penny. Each of these had (and still has) a deep cellar where French and Rhenish wines could easily be stacked. In the medieval vaulted cellars of Taverne Curiosa (Vlamingstraat 22), the alcohol-laden atmosphere of those bygone days can still be inhaled. Halfway along Vlamingstraat is the elegant City Theatre 41 on your left. This royal theatre (1869) is one of Europe's best-preserved city theatres. Behind the Neo-Renaissance façade lie a magnifi-

TIP

Since as long ago as 1897, two green painted mobile chippies have stood in front of the Belfry. It is definitely the best place in town to buy – and sell – chips, good for the annual consumption of several tons of fast food! The stalls are open nearly every hour of the day and night, so that you never need to go hungry!

Vlamingstraat

SWANS ON THE CANALS

After the death of the much-loved Mary of Burgundy (1482), Bruges went through some troubled times. The townspeople, enraged by new taxes Maximilian of Austria, Mary's successor, had imposed upon them, rose in revolt against their new ruler. As Maximilian was locked up in House Craenenburg (Markt 16), he helplessly witnessed the torture and eventual beheading of his bailiff and trusted councillor Pieter Lanchals (Long Neck) on the Markt. A stubborn old legend says that when the duke came back to power, he took his vengeance on the local people by forcing them to keep 'long necks' or swans on the canals for all time. In reality, however, swans have been on the canals since the beginning of the 15th century, when they were seen as a status symbol of the city's power and wealth.

cent auditorium and a palatial foyer. Papageno, the bird seller from Mozart's opera, *The Magic Flute*, guards the entrance. His score lies scattered on the square opposite.

Continue along Vlamingstraat and turn right into Kortewinkel just before the water.

41

Somewhat hidden from gazing eyes, Kortewinkel boasts a unique 16th-century wooden house front. It is one of only two left in the city (you will come across the other one further along this walk). Just a few metres on is another exciting discovery at number 10. The former Jesuit House 09 has a magnificent hidden courtyard garden. Is its door open? Then walk in and enjoy its heavenly peace.

Kortewinkel turns into Spaanse Loskaai, the home port of the Spanish merchants until the end of the 16th century.

At 700 years of age, the picturesque bridge you pass on the left, the Augustijnenbrug (Augustinians' Bridge), is one of the oldest in Bruges. The stone seats were originally intended to display the wares of the diligent sellers. The bridge affords an excellent view of the house in the right-hand corner, which connects Spanjaardstraat with Kortewinkel. This was once House De Noodt Gods but is also said to be a haunted house, according to the locals. When an amorous monk was rejected by a nun, the man murdered her and then committed suicide. Ever since they have been haunting that ramshackle building...

Continue along Spaanse Loskaai, go down the first street on your right and proceed to Oosterlingenplein.
During Bruges' golden century, this was the fixed abode of the so-called 'Oosterlingen' (Easteners) or German merchants. Their imposing warehouse took up the entire left corner of the square. Today the only remnant is the building to the right of Hotel Bryghia. Their warehouse must have been truly grand!

Beyond Oosterlingenplein is Woensdagmarkt, the square on which the statue of the painter Hans Memling attracts all attention. Turn right into Genthof.

Genthof

Here the second of two authentic medieval wooden house fronts draws attention. Notice that each floor juts out a little more than the previous one. This building technique, which helped to avoid water damage (but also created extra space), was consequently used in various architectural styles.

Burgundian Manhattan

Proceed to Jan van Eyckplein.
This was the Manhattan of Burgundian Bruges, the place where everything happened. It was here that ships moored, were loaded and unloaded, and paid their tolls. In this unremitting hustle and bustle, a cacophony of languages was heard above the din, one sounding even louder than the other. What a soundtrack! Each business transaction required a few local sounds too, of course, as there always had to be a Bruges broker present who would naturally pocket his cut. On the corner, the 16th-century House De Rode Steen (number 8) has been sparkling in all its glory since its restora-

TIP

The Genthof has in recent years attracted a variety of different arts and crafts. There is a glass-blower, a trendy vintage store and a number of contemporary art galleries. And on the corner with Langerei, you can find 't Terrastje, the café with probably the smallest terrace in Bruges.

Jan Van Eyckplein (left: House De Rode Steen)

tion (the first building in Bruges to be renovated thanks to a subsidy from the city) in 1877. At numbers 1-2 is the Old Tollhouse (1477) 05 22. It was the place where tolls were levied on the goods and products of both regional and international trade. On the left-hand side of this truly monumental building stands the Rijkepijnders House, the smallest house in Bruges. This was the meeting place of the *rijkepijnders*, the agents who supervised the porters, and the dockworkers employed to load and unload the ships. People with sharp eyes may be able to spot some of these heavily laden *pijnders* depicted on the facade.

Continue along Academiestraat.
Right on the corner with Jan van Eyckplein is another remarkable building, distinguished by its striking tower. This is the Burghers' Lodge (Poortersloge) 16, a 15th-century building where the burgesses of the city (patricians and merchants) once used to meet. In a wall niche, the Bruges Bear, an important city symbol, stands proud and upright. From 1720 to 1890, the Burghers' Lodge was the home of the Municipal Academy of Fine Arts, whose collection later formed the basis for the Groeninge Museum. From 1912 to 2012, the building served as the home of the State Archives.

Proceed to Grauwwerkersstraat. The little square connecting Academiestraat with Grauwwerkersstraat has been known as 'Beursplein' since time immemorial.
Here merchants were engaged in high-quality trade. The merchant houses of Genoa (Genuese Lodge, later renamed 'Saaihalle' 08 and today the Belgian

THE LITTLE BEAR OF BRUGES

When Baldwin Iron Arm, the first Count of Flanders, visited Bruges for the first time, the first creature he saw was a huge, snow-covered brown bear. According to the legend, all this happened in the 9th century. After a fierce fight, the count succeeded in killing the animal. In homage to the courageous beast, he proclaimed the bear to be the city's very own symbol. Today 'Bruges' oldest inhabitant' in the niche of the Burghers' Lodge is festively rigged out during exceptional celebrations. The Bruges Bear is holding the coat of arms of the Noble Company of the White Bear, a chivalric order of knights famed for their jousting tournaments, which was founded shortly after Baldwin I had beaten the 'white' bear and which held its meetings in the Burghers' Lodge.

Fries Museum 21), Florence (now De Florentijnen restaurant) and Venice (now pool bar The Monk) once stood here side by side like brothers. In front of house Ter Beurse (1276) 11, the central inn, merchants from all over Europe used to gather to arrange business appointments and conduct exchange transactions. The Dutch word for stock exchange became 'beurs', derived from the name of the house. Many other languages would take over this term, such as French (bourse) or Italian (borsa).

08 11 21

Turn into Grauwwerkersstraat and stop immediately in your tracks.
The side wall of house Ter Beurse 11, and more precisely the part between the two sets of ground-floor windows, bears the signatures of the stonecutters. This way, everybody knew which mason cut which stones and how much each mason had to be paid. The house next-door to house Ter Beurse, called 'de Kleine Beurse' (the Little Stock Exchange), still sits on its original street level.

Turn left into Naaldenstraat.
On your right, Bladelin Court 09 with its attractive tower looms up ahead. Pieter Bladelin, portrayed above the

PRINSENHOF GOSSIP

> As Philip the Good hadn't yet laid eyes on his future wife (Isabella of Portugal), he sent Jan van Eyck to Portugal to paint her portrait. This way the duke wanted to make certain he had made the right choice. The duke's ploy worked, because history teaches us that the couple had a happy marriage.
> Although the popular Mary of Burgundy incurred only seemingly minor injuries as a result of a fall with her horse, the accident would eventually lead to her death from a punctured lung at Prinsenhof. Back in those times there was no cure for inflammation.
> During the hotel renovation, no fewer than 578 silver coins, minted between 1755 and 1787, were dug up. After some careful counting and calculations, it is assumed that the energetic English nuns, who lived there at that time, entrusted the coins to the soil so as to prevent the advancing French troops from stealing their hard-earned capital.

gate whilst praying to the Virgin Mary, first rented out and then sold his mansion to the Florentine banking family, the Medici, who ran a branch of their bank here in the 15th century. Today, this property is owned by the Sisters of Our Lady of the Seven Sorrows.

Somewhat further along, next to another ornamental tower, turn right into Boterhuis, a winding cobbled alley that catapults you back straight into the Middle Ages. Keep right, pass Saint James's Church and turn left into Moerstraat.

The Dukes of Burgundy and the vast majority of foreign merchants patronised Saint James's Church 22. Their extrav-

TIP

Behind the street Boterhuis, at Sint-Jakobsstraat 26, you will find Cinema Lumière 15, purveyor of the better kind of artistic film. In other words, the place to be for real film lovers.

09

agant gifts have left their glittering mark on the interior.

Prinsenhof (the Princes' Court), home base of the Dukes of Burgundy

Turn left into Geerwijnstraat and carry on to Muntplein.

Muntplein (Coin Square) belonged to nearby Prinsenhof 17. As you might have guessed, this was where Bruges' mint was situated. The statue *Flandria Nostra* (Our Flanders), which represents a noblewoman on horseback, was designed by the Belgian sculptor Jules Lagae (1862-1931).

At the end of Geerwijnstraat, turn right into Geldmuntstraat. The walk's finishing point is Prinsenhof.

We end the walk on a highlight. Prinsenhof used to be the palace of the Flemish counts and Burgundy dukes. This impressive mansion, originally seven times the size of what you see today, was expanded in the 15th century by Philip the Good to celebrate his (third) marriage to Isabella of Portugal. When Charles the Bold remarried Margaret of York, the largest bathhouse in Europe, a game court (to play 'jeu de paume' or the palm game, the forerunner of tennis) and a zoological garden were all added to the ducal residence. It is no surprise that Prinsenhof not only became the favourite pied-à-terre of the Dukes of Burgundy, but also the nerve centre of their political, econom-

17

ic and cultural ambitions. Both Philip the Good (d.1467) and Mary of Burgundy (d.1482) breathed their last here. After the death of the popular Mary of Burgundy, the palace's fortunes declined, until it eventually ended up in private hands. In the 17th century, English nuns converted it into a boarding school for girls of well-to-do parents. Nowadays, you can stay in the Prinsenhof Castle in true princely style.

TIP

Whoever wants to get a really good impression of the magnificence of this city castle and its elegant gardens should follow the signs in the Ontvangersstraat to the hotel car park at Moerstraat 46. Of course, you can always treat yourself – and your nearest and dearest – to a princely drink in the bar of the hotel: the perfect way to enjoy the grandeur and luxury of the complex.

Walk 3

Strolling through silent Bruges

Ramparts

Although the city quarters of Saint Anne and Saint Giles are known as places of great tranquillity, the fact that they are off the beaten track does not mean that the visitor will be short of adventure. How about a row of nostalgic windmills? Or perhaps some unpretentious working-class neighbourhoods, or a couple of exclusive gentlemen's clubs? Will you be able to take in all these impressions? Don't worry. After the tour we invite you to catch your breath in Bruges' oldest cafe!

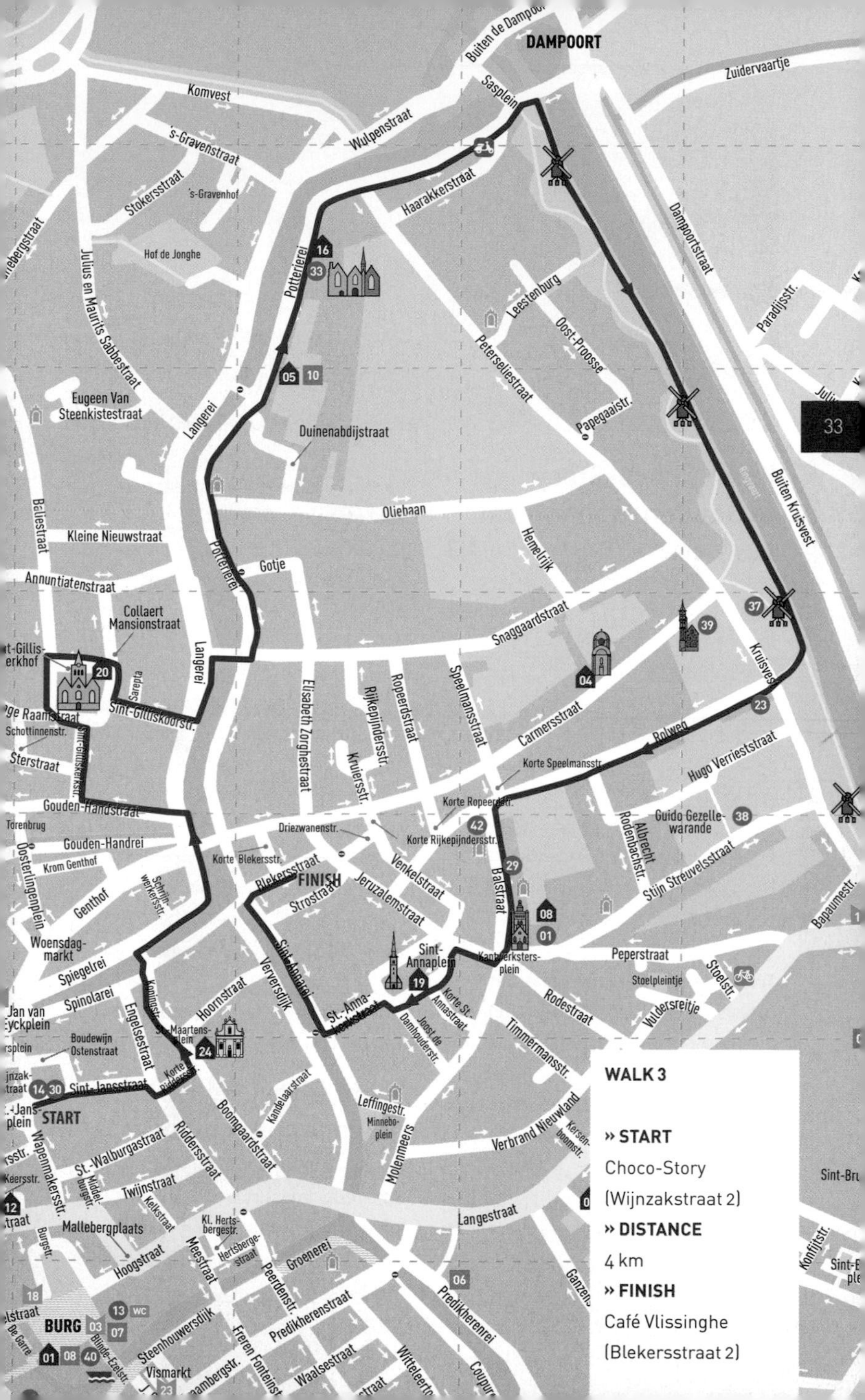

WALK 3

» START

Choco-Story (Wijnzakstraat 2)

» DISTANCE

4 km

» FINISH

Café Vlissinghe (Blekersstraat 2)

Koningsbrug

From Choco-Story to Gouden-Handstraat

Choco-Story (Chocolate Museum) 14 is the perfect starting point for the longest walk in this guide. This museum not only dips you in the yummy history of chocolate and cocoa, it also offers extensive chocolate tasting. If you wish, you can also buy your supplies here. No doubt the chocolate will help you keep up a brisk pace! At the same address, Lumina Domestica 30 contains the world's largest collection of lamps and lights. The museum also houses six thousand antiques.

Turn left into Sint-Jansstraat, carry on to Korte Riddersstraat and continue until the end of the street.

The impressive Saint Walburga's Church 24 rises up in all its magnificence right in front of you. This outstanding Baroque edifice (1619-1642) boasts a remarkable marble communion rail and high altar. Nearby, at number 5 there is a splendid 18th-century mansion.

Continue down Koningstraat to the bridge.

This bridge, which connects poetic Spinolarei with Spiegelrei, offers you a beautiful view on your left of the Jan van Eyck square *(read more in Walk 2, on pages 27-28)*. At Spiegelrei 3 you can admire the remarkable Oud Huis Amsterdam, a historic mansion that nowadays houses a high-class hotel. This part of the city used to be mainly populated by the English and Scots. The English merchants even had their own 'steegere', or stair where their goods were unloaded. The stair is still there, and the street connecting it is appropriately called Engelsestraat. The dignified white school building (Spiegelrei 15) across the bridge was once a college of English Jesuits.

Saint Giles', home base of workmen and artists

Cross the bridge, turn right along Spiegelrei and turn into Gouden-Handstraat, the fourth street on your left.

In the 15th century, Gouden-Handstraat and the parish of Saint Giles were known as the artists' quarter. Hans Memling may have lived a few streets further down in Sint-Jorisstraat; the fact of the matter is that Jan van Eyck had a studio in Gouden-Handstraat, and that his somewhat lesser-known fellow artists also used to congregate in this neighbourhood.

Turn right into Sint-Gilliskerkstraat.
This street bumps into Saint Giles' Church 20 in the heart of the tranquil quarter of Saint Giles'. Initially a chapel, this building was upgraded to a parish church in 1258. In spite of its interior in Gothic revival style and its superb paintings, the church takes on the appearance of a simple, sturdy village church. Don't be misled. In and around the church countless famous painters were buried, such as Hans Memling (d.1494), in his time the best-paid painter, Lanceloot Blondeel (d.1561) and Pieter Pourbus (d.1584). Their graves and the cemetery may have disappeared, but their artists' souls still hover in the air.

Walk around the church and turn into Sint-Gilliskoorstraat.
Although the workmen's dwellings in these streets are rather small, they nevertheless display a bricked-up window. As it happened, a tax on windows was levied in 1800. Consequently, a large number of windows were walled up.

From Potterierei to the 'vesten' (ramparts)

Turn left into Langerei at the end of the street. Cross the lovely Snaggaardbrug, the first bridge you get to, into Potterierei. Turn left and follow the canal for some time.

Woensdagmarkt

20

BRUGES AND THE SEA

For centuries, Langerei ensured the city's wealth. This canal ran to Damme, where it was connected to a large lock, called 'Speie', which in turn was connected to the Zwin, a deep sea channel and tidal inlet. While Damme developed into an outport, Bruges grew into Northwestern Europe's greatest business centre of the Middle Ages. The arts flourished, culture thrived, prosperity seemed to be set for all eternity. The tide turned when Mary of Burgundy suddenly passed away in 1482. The relations between Bruges and the Burgundians turned sour and the Burgundian court left the city. The foreign merchants and their wealth followed in its wake. The Zwin continued to silt up and Bruges lost her privileged commercial position. As a result, and compounded by a series of political intrigues, the city fell into a deep winter sleep.

After a fair distance along Potterierei is Bruges' Major Seminary (number 72) 05 on your right. A unique place with a lush orchard and meadows with cows at pasture. Between 1628 and 1642, a new Cistercian Abbey (the Dune Abbey) was erected here, which later on would achieve great fame for the wealth and erudition of its occupants. During the French Revolution, the abbey was brought under public ownership, and the abbot and monks were chased away. The 17th-century abbey buildings were first used as a military hospital and then as a military depot and a grammar school before they were

eventually taken over by the Major Seminary in 1833, where Catholic priests received their religious instruction until 2018. Today, the Major Seminary serves as an educational and training facility for the diocese. There is also a research and training centre for the University of the United Nations 10. Just a few yards further down at number 79B is Our Lady of the Pottery 16 33. Its history goes back to the 13th century. Diligent nuns used to treat pilgrims, travellers and the sick here. From the 15th century onwards, it became a home for the care of the elderly. The Gothic church with its Baroque interior and its rich collection of works of art, accumulated by the hospital throughout the centuries, is a hidden gem that is certainly well worth a visit!

Carry on to the lock and spend some time by the water.

This idyllic spot is where the canal Damse Vaart heads out across the other side of the ring road towards the equally romantic town of Damme. It's hard to believe that this area around the canal was once a scene of great controversy. Up until the Eighty Years' War, Bruges was connected to the Dutch town of Sluis by way of Damme. Ambitious Napoleon Bonaparte had the connection to the tidal inlet of the Zwin, the natural predecessor of the Damse Vaart, dredged by Spanish prisoners of war so as to create a watercourse that would run all the way to Antwerp. His plan then was to develop the port city of

TIP

Have we sparked your curiosity? Or do you just like to do things the easy way? If so, leave your bike and car at home and jump aboard for a voyage on the Lamme Goedzak the most stylish way to reach the town of Damme. Step back in time during this nostalgic journey.
(For more information see page 51.)

Antwerp into a naval base, which would enable him to avoid the English sea blockade. Napoleon's project left Damme cut in twain. The wild plans of the little general were never carried out in full, and by 1814 Napoleon's role in Flanders had come to an end. Under

Sasplein

the impulse of William I, King of the Netherlands, who also saw the value of a connecting canal, the digging work continued until 1824. Belgian independence (1830) meant that the project was finally terminated, by which time it had reached as far as Sluis. Today the low traffic bicycle path skirting the canal is a most attractive route linking Bruges with Damme. The trip is highly recommended, as it traverses *le plat pays*, that flat country made famous by Jacques Brel. Imagine! In the middle of a unique polder landscape this truly poetic canal strip, bordered by lofty poplars bended down by eternal westerly winds.

Turn right and carry on along the Vesten (ramparts), which surround the city like a ring of green.

In the 16th century, more than thirty windmills were turning their sails here. Today only four are left. In the 18th century, the millers stood by helplessly when bread consumption took a dive and people started to consume more potatoes. Eventually steam machines would take over the millers' tasks. One of the mills, the Sint-Janshuis Mill 37, can still be visited today. A miller will be happy not only to give you an explanation of his craft, but will also show you how the milling is done. It is well worth climbing the slopes on which the Sint-

THE ARCHERS' GUILD: 120 MEN AND 2 QUEENS!

39

Two centuries-old archery clubs are now to be found in what was one of the poorer districts of Bruges in the 19th century. High and dry on the same hill as the Sint-Janshuis Mill, at the bottom left, stands the Sint-Joris (St. George's) Guild 38, a crossbow guild that specializes in two archery disciplines: shooting at targets on the ground and shooting at feathered discs in a tower. To the right, with its eye-catching target tower, is the home of the Sint-Sebastiaan (St. Sebastian) Guild 39, a longbow society. This guild goes back more than six centuries, which makes it unique in the world. The society numbers about 120 male members and two notable female honorary members: the Belgian queen Mathilde and the British queen. Ever since the exiled English king Charles II took up residence in Bruges in the 17th century, the city and the British Royal Family have always been closely associated. Within the St. Sebastian Archery Guild, Charles founded both the British Grenadier Guards and the Life Guards Regiment. To visit the St. Sebastian Guild, make an appointment via www.sebastiaansgilde.be.

37

Janshuis Mill and the Bonne Chiere Mill (near the Kruispoort/Cross Gate 12) proudly stand. From the top of these mill mounds, there is a fantastic panoramic view across the city. This is the perfect spot to brush up on your amassed knowledge of Bruges. And there's more! Down below on your right is the Verloren Hoek (the Lost Corner), now an authentic working-class district, but back in the 19th century an impoverished neighbourhood with such a bad reputation that even the police didn't dare enter its streets.

TIP

Interested in a little something 'extra'? Then go and take a look at the Albrecht Rodenbachstraat, another of the city's hidden gems. This green suburb avant la lettre offers an almost unbroken succession of stepgables and other fascinating facades, each fronted by a delightful little garden.

Silent Bruges

Descend down the slope and turn right into Rolweg.

Right on the corner is the Gezelle Museum 23, the birthplace of Guido Gezelle (1830-1899), one of Flanders' most venerable poets. On display are handwritten letters, writing material and a deliciously peaceful garden with an age-old Corsican pine. Gezelle's parents worked here as gardener and caretaker, in exchange for which they and their family received free board and lodging. Little Guido grew up in these idyllic surroundings. He would eventually return to Bruges many years later and after many a peregrination. Upon his return, he became curate of Saint Walburga's Church 24. He also took over the running of the English Convent 04, where he would die. These were his last words, reportedly: *'I have so*

TIP

If you feel like taking a break, you are welcome to rest your tired feet in the large, walled garden of the Museum of Folk Life 42. It is a delightful oasis of calm in the heart of the city, and even has its own outdoor pétanque alley! At Balstraat 16, you can visit the Lace Centre 29, which has been installed in the fully renovated old lace school. If you visit during one of the many lace demonstrations (2.00-5.00 p.m., not on Sundays and public holidays), it will immediately strike you how popular lacemaking still is today, both with young and old alike.

loved hearing the birds singing.' Here, in this most verdant part of Bruges, we still know precisely what the priest and poet meant.

Turn into Balstraat, the second street on the left.

This picturesque working-man's alley houses the Museum of Folk Life (Volkskundemuseum) 42. The 17th-century row of almshouses, restored and converted into authentic artisans' interiors such as a milliner's, a confectioner's and a small classroom, will take you back to bygone days. The tower of the 15th-century Jerusalem Chapel 08 can easily be spotted from these premises. This chapel was com-

01 08

19

29

missioned by the Adornes, a prominent Bruges merchant family of Genoese origin, who lived in a magnificent mansion 01 on the Peperstraat. In 1470, Anselm Adornes collected one of his sons (the father had no fewer than sixteen children) in Padua to set off on a pilgrimage to the Holy Land. Upon his return to Bruges, Anselm decided to build an exact copy of the Church of the Holy Sepulchre. The result was remarkable. In the adjacent Adornes Estate 01, you will make closer acquaintance with this prominent family and its intriguing history.

At the crossroads, turn right into Jeruzalemstraat; then, at the church, left onto Sint-Annaplein.

The tiny square is dominated by the apparently simple Church of Saint Anne 19. Its exterior may be austere, but its interior is one of Bruges' most splendid examples of Baroque architecture. As this neighbourhood gradually became more prestigious, the church did the same!

With the church behind you, follow the Sint-Annakerkstraat and then turn right into Sint-Annarei.

At the corner of the confluence of the two waterways, one of Bruges' most handsome town houses is proudly showing off its Rococo credentials (Sint-Annarei no. 22). Sit yourself down on a bench in the shadow and enjoy this exceptional view.

Retrace your steps for just a few yards and turn left into Blekersstraat next to the bridge.

Café Vlissinghe at number 2 is undoubtedly Bruges' oldest café. This has been a tavern since 1515. It is no surprise then that you will find oodles of ambiance here. It is therefore the perfect place to settle down and let the wonderful memories of your walk slowly sink in. A local beer will be your ideal companion. Cheers!

History in a nutshell

Although the Bruges region was already populated in Roman times, the city's name appears for the first time in the 9th century, probably derived from the Old Germanic word 'brugj', which means 'mooring'. Bruges has always had a special bond with the sea. After all, water played a crucial role in the city's foundation. It was the place where several streams merged into a single river (the 'Reie'), which flowed north into the coastal plain. This river was linked to the North Sea through a series of 'tidal channels', guaranteeing the city's future welfare and prosperity.

In the early Middle Ages, Bruges developed into an international and bustling trading city with its own port, made possible by its favourable location and connection with the sea. At the same time, the fortified town became a powerful political stronghold, thanks to the presence of the Flemish Counts, who ruled over the County of Flanders. In the 13th century, Bruges was the leading trade centre of northwestern Europe. Merchants from all over Europe settled in the city and the world's first ever stock exchange ('Beurs' in Dutch) was founded in Bruges. These market activities took place in front of the house owned by a powerful family of brokers, the Van der Beurse family. As a result, their name became linked for all time with this kind of financial institution. In spite of the typical medieval maladies, the citizens of Bruges prospered, and soon the city developed a magnet-like radiation. Around 1340, the inner city numbered no fewer than 35.000 inhabitants.

The golden century

The success continued and in the 15th century, Bruges' golden century, business was better than ever before. This was due to the fact that since the end of the 14th century Flanders was now part of the realms of the dukes of Burgundy. They expanded their presence in Bruges, turning the city into a cultural and commercial centre that was second to none. In addition to the traditional broadcloth, numerous new luxury goods were now produced and sold. Famous painters such as Jan van Eyck and Hans Memling – the great Flemish primitives – found their creative niche here. The fine arts flourished, and in addition to wonderful churches and unique 'nation houses' (embassies), the monumental town hall was also completed. Bruges' success seemed imperishable.

Market Square, 17th century;
with the long since vanished Water Halls on the left

Burg, 17th century, with the long since vanished St. Donatian's Cathedral on the left and the former facade of the Palace of the Liberty of Bruges in the centre.

Both paintings by Jan-Baptist Meunincxhove can be seen in the Town Hall on the Burg.

Decline

The sudden death in 1482 of the much-loved ruler, Mary of Burgundy, heralded the start of new and less fortunate times for the city. The relationship between the citizens of Bruges and their lord, the widower Maximilian of Austria, turned sour. The Burgundian court left the city, with the international traders following in its wake. To make matters worse, Bruges' connection with the sea quickly silted up. The Golden Age had passed and was succeeded by long eras of war and regime change. By the time Belgium gained independence (1830), Bruges was a poor and impoverished provincial city. Strangely enough, its fortunes were changed for the better by the writing of a novel.

Revival

In *Bruges la Morte* (1892), Georges Rodenbach aptly describes Bruges as a somewhat sleepy, yet extremely mysterious place. In particular, the 35 pictures that were included in the book for illustrative purposes sparked his readers' curiosity. Soon Bruges' magnificent patrimony was rediscovered and its mysterious intimacy turned out to be its greatest asset. With great care, Bruges took its first steps into tourism. The age-old desire to be connected with the sea resulted in the development of a new international seaport at the end of the 19th century, which was given the name of Zeebrugge.

Bruges today

During the First World War, Zeebrugge became the operational base for the German submarine fleet, coordinated from their headquarters on the market square in Bruges. Fortunately, both world wars left the historic city centre virtually unscathed, making Bruges increasingly appealing to visitors and culture-lovers alike. Its beauty and attraction was confirmed in 2000, when UNESCO classified the entire medieval inner city as a world heritage site. The rest, as they say, is history.

Rozenhoedkaai

Know your way around **Bruges**

Exploring Bruges

The canals of Bruges

Admittedly, it's great to wander aimlessly through the winding streets of Bruges. But it's also fun to explore the city more actively. And there are lots of ways you can do this: a guided walk or a bike ride past many secret spots, a boat trip on the mysterious canals or a romantic drive in horse-drawn carriage. If you prefer a quick and comfortable view of the city's highlights, perhaps a minibus tour is the thing for you. Fancy a more thrilling experience? So why not see the city while running? Alternatively, you can choose a modern Segway or make an unforgettable balloon flight. There's something for everyone!

TWO EXCURSIONS YOU DON'T WANT TO MISS

MYSTERIOUS CANALS AND THE RHYTHMIC CLOPPING OF HOOVES

The canals of Bruges – the 'reien' – are the arteries of the city. Nothing is as pleasant as chugging along in a boat as you sail past all the most beautiful places in the city. From the 'reien', you discover hidden romantic corners and secret gardens. There are regular daily sailings from any of the five moorings in the heart of the city. A voyage lasts half an hour.

Or why not opt for a coach ride over centuries-old squares and charming bridges of the historic city centre. For half an hour, you can sit back and enjoy the rhythmic clopping of horse's hooves as you take in all the most picturesque spots in Bruges. During your ride the coachman will give you an expert commentary and about half way you make a short stop at the Beguinage.

Bruges by boat

OPEN > Sailings guaranteed from March to mid-November: in principle, daily, 10.00 a.m.-6.00 p.m., last sailing at 5.30 p.m.
PRICE > €10; children aged 4 to 11: €6; children under 4: free

Bruges by horse-drawn carriage

OPEN > Daily, 9.00 a.m. to at least 6.00 p.m., but no later than 10.00 p.m.
PRICE PER CARRIAGE > €50; max. 5 people
MEETING POINT > Markt, but at the Burg square on Wednesday morning
INFO > www.hippo.be/koets

Bruges by bus

City Tour Bruges

City Tour's minibuses offer a top-quality 50-minute tour past Bruges' most delightful spots and key places of interest.

OPEN > Daily, every half hour (also on public holidays). The first bus leaves at 10.00 a.m. The last bus leaves:

> at 4.00 p.m. during the period 1/11 to 31/1
> at 4.30 p.m. during the period 1/2 to 9/2
> at 5.00 p.m. during the period 10/2 to 28/2
> at 5.30 p.m. during the periods 1/3 to 15/3 and 16/10 to 31/10
> at 6.00 p.m. during the periods 16/3 to 30/4 and 1/10 to 15/10
> at 7.00 p.m. during the period 1/5 to 30/9

There are no departures at 6.30 p.m.

ADDITIONAL CLOSING DATE > 15/9

PRICE > Including headphones with explanation (available in 16 languages): €20; children aged 6 to 11 years: €15; children under 6: free

MEETING POINT > Markt

INFO > www.citytour.be

Photo Tour Brugge

Whether you are a photography expert or a novice, during the Photo Tour Andy McSweeney takes you to all the most photogenic spots in the city.

OPEN > Daily: *Edges of Brugge* (10.00 a.m.-12.00 p.m.) focuses on the side streets and canals; *Essential Brugge* (1.00 p.m.-3.00 p.m.) zooms in on the top sights; during *Hidden Brugge* (4.00 p.m.-6.00 p.m.) you will go in search of some of the city's less well-known corners; the private tour *Shades of Brugge* (8.00 p.m.-11.00 p.m.) allows you to experience the evening delights of the city.

PRICE > €60 (max. 5 photographers per tour); private tour: €220 (max. 3 photographers); each participating photographer can bring along a non-photographer free of charge. Prior reservation is necessary, but is possible on the day.

MEETING POINT > Basilica of the Holy Blood, on the Burg square

LANGUAGES > English, but on request also Dutch and/or French

INFO > Tel. +32 (0)486 17 52 75, www.phototourbrugge.com

Bruges by heart

Top-quality walk with local guides

During this exclusive walk (max. 16 people), a city guide will take you on a fascinating journey. Not only will you discover many of the great historic buildings and sites, but also some hidden gems and secret places. The walk starts with a breathtaking view of the city from the roof terrace of the Concert Hall. A unique experience!

OPEN > Find out via www.visitbruges.be when you can book a place on one of the walks or pop into one of the tourist offices.
PRICE > (Subject to amendment) €12.50; children under 12 years: free
MEETING POINT > The walk starts from the tourist office 't Zand (Concert Hall)
LANGUAGES > English, Dutch, French. During certain periods, also in German.
TICKETS > Tourist offices Markt (Historium) and 't Zand (Concert Hall) or via www.ticketsbrugge.be
APP > Another way to explore the city on foot (or by bike) is to use the free Xplore Bruges app. *You can find more info on www.xplorebruges.be and on page 98.*
INFO > Tel. +32 (0)50 44 46 46, www.visitbruges.be

Running around Bruges

Tourist Run Brugge – guided tours

Accompanied by a guide you run – at a gentle pace – through the streets and alleyways of Bruges. The circuit, which ends on the Markt, is 9.5 km long. With the explanation that you receive along the way, you should allow 1 to 1.30 hours for completion.

OPEN > Daily, tours at 7.00 a.m., 8.00 a.m., 9.00 a.m., 5.00 p.m., 6.00 p.m., 7.00 p.m., 8.00 p.m. and 9.00 p.m. Reservation is required.
PRICE > €30/person; for 2 runners: €25/person; 3 runners or more: €20/person
MEETING POINT > At the statue of Jan Breydel and Pieter de Coninck on the Markt. If requested in advance, you can be picked up from wherever you are staying (hotel, etc.).
LANGUAGES > English, Dutch, French, German
INFO > Tel. +32 (0)483 49 15 74, www.touristrunbrugge.be

Bruges by bike

QuasiMundo Biketours: Bruges by bike

Riding through the narrow streets, you will discover the charming character of Bruges. The fascinating stories of the guide will catapult you back in time to the era when counts and dukes ruled over the city. During the trip you will cross almost the entire city.
OPEN > 1/3 to 31/12: daily, 10.00 a.m.-12.30 p.m. Reservation is required.
PRICE > Including bike and raincoat: €30 or €28 (youngsters aged 9 to 26); if

you bring your own bike: €18 or €16 (youngsters aged 9 to 26); children under 9: free
MEETING POINT > Predikherenstraat 28, 10 min. before departure
LANGUAGES > English, but also Dutch, French and German on request
INFO > Tel. +32 (0)50 33 07 75 or +32 (0)478 28 15 21, www.quasimundo.eu
(Also see 'Guided tours through Bruges' wood- and wetlands', page 142.)

Bruges by bike carriage

Fietskoetsen Brugge
Discover all the city's most romantic places and historical sites of interest in a unique and ecological way. A personal guide will take you on a bike carriage tour of 30 minutes.
OPEN > 1/1 to 30/4 and 1/11 to 15/12: on Saturday and Sunday, 11.00 a.m.-5.00 p.m., other moments by appointment only; 1/5 to 31/10 and 16/12 to 31/12: Tuesday to Sunday, 10.00 a.m.-6.00 p.m.
PRICE PER BIKE CARRIAGE > €24; max. 3 people
MEETING POINT > On the Markt, outside the Burger King; but on the Burg square on Wednesday mornings
LANGUAGES > English, Dutch, French, Spanish
INFO > Tel. +32 (0)478 40 95 57, www.fietskoetsenbrugge.be

Bruges on a Segway

Segway Brugge
An original way to explore the city without having to walk! After a short initi-

ation, a personal guide takes you on a route past the historic sites, monuments, unique buildings and hidden treasures of Bruges. You can also opt for a chocolate, *Bruges by night*, dinner or brewery tour.
OPEN > Daily, tours at 10.00 a.m., 12.00 p.m., 2.00 p.m., 4.00 p.m. and 6.00 p.m.
PRICE > Standard tour: €40 (1 hour) or €55 (2 hours), other tours are more expensive. Prior reservation is necessary, but is possible on the day itself (min. 2 people).
LANGUAGES > English, Dutch, French, German
INFO AND MEETING POINT > Oud Sint-Jan site, Zonnekemeers 18, tel. +32 (0)50 68 87 70 or +32 (0)495 90 60 60, www.segwaybrugge.be

Bruges by hot air balloon

Bruges Ballooning
The most adventurous and probably the most romantic way to discover Bruges is by hot air balloon. Bruges Ballooning organizes both a morning flight and an evening flight over Bruges. The whole trip lasts for three hours, with at least one hour in the air.

OPEN > 1/4 to 31/10: daily flights, but only if booked in advance; bookings can be made on the day.
PRICE > €180; children aged 4 to 12: €110
MEETING POINT > You will be picked up and dropped off wherever you are staying.
LANGUAGES > English, Dutch, French, Spanish
INFO > Tel. +32 (0)475 97 28 87, www.bruges-ballooning.com

Lamme Goedzak (steam wheeler) Damme

The nostalgic river boat 'Lamme Goedzak' sails four times a day back and forth between Bruges and the centre of Damme.
OPEN > Tuesday to Saturday during Easter holiday and 1/5 to 30/9: departures from Bruges to Damme at 12.00 p.m., 2.00 p.m., 4.00 p.m. and 6.00 p.m.; departures from Damme to Bruges at 11.00 a.m., 1.00 p.m., 3.00 p.m. and 5.00 p.m.
PRICE > €10.50 (one-way ticket) or €14.50 (return ticket); 65+: €10 (one-way ticket) or €12.50 (return ticket); children aged 3 to 11: €9 (one-way ticket) or €11.50 (return ticket). Tickets can only be purchased on the boat.
MEETING POINT > Embark in Bruges at the Noorweegse Kaai 31 (City map: J1). Embarkation in Damme: Damse Vaart-Zuid
INFO > Tel. +32 (0)50 28 86 10, www.bootdamme-brugge.be

Port Cruise Zeebrugge

The 75-minute port cruise takes in the naval base, the Pierre Vandamme Lock (one of the largest locks in the world), the gas terminal, the wind turbine park, the 'tern' island, the cruise ships and the dredging vessels. You will also see how the massive container ships are unloaded at the quay. A unique experience!
OPEN > 1/4 to 13/10: weekends and public holidays round trip at 2.00 p.m.; 1/7 to 31/8: daily round trip at 2.00 p.m. and 4.00 p.m.; 1/8 to 15/8: daily extra round trip at 11.00 a.m.
PRICE > On board: €12.50; 60+: €11.50; children aged 3 to 11: €10. Tickets can also be purchased online at a reduced price.
MEETING POINT > Embark at the landing stage at the end of the Tijdokstraat (old fishing port), Zeebrugge
LANGUAGES > English, Dutch, French, German. You can also download the commentary on your smartphone (free).
INFO > Tel. +32 (0)59 70 62 94 (for extra departures outside the fixed sailing times), www.franlis.be

Museums, places of interest and attractions

Shrine of Saint Ursula (Saint John's Hospital)

Bruges has many unique places that you simply must see, each one an atmospheric testimony to the city's rich history. The Flemish primitives are undoubtedly Bruges' showpiece attraction, including Hans Memling's *Shrine of Saint Ursula* and Jan van Eyck's *Madonna with Canon Joris van der Paele*. Even so, museum devotees in search of much more will not be disappointed. Indeed, the Bruges range of attractions is truly magnificent. From modern plastic art by way of Michelangelo's world-famous *Madonna and Child* to the Lace Centre. It's all there for you to discover!

IN THE SPOTLIGHT

GRUUTHUSE MUSEUM REOPENS
A PALACE FULL OF WONDERS

One of Bruges' most inspiring and evocative buildings is the historical Gruuthuse Palace, where the lords of Gruuthuse once resided in great splendour. Following a long period of renovation, the luxurious 15th century city palace will reopen its doors in the course of 2019. The family motto *'Plus est en vous'*, which translates as 'There is more in you (than you think)', proudly stands above the entrance. The results of the renovation are as impressive on the inside as they are on the outside. The new Gruuthuse Museum will amaze its visitors. The many (spiral) staircases and the succession of large and small rooms turn the museum route into a thrilling voyage of discovery. Ancient artefacts give new meaning to 500 years of Bruges history and introduce you to the city's elite, its skilled craftsmen and artists, and their quest for the ultimate in refinement and prestige.

But it is not only the palace that has been thoroughly refurbished. The romantic courtyard has also been given a makeover, with the addition of a glass pavilion that will serve as a central information point and ticket counter for both the Gruuthuse Museum and the adjacent Church of Our Lady. The pavilion forms a unique bridge between old and new, whilst at the same time restoring the former intimate and closed nature of the original courtyard. It is also the ideal location to acquire your Musea Brugge Card. *(Read more on pages 64, 67 and 75.)*

01 08 Adornesdomein – Jeruzalemkapel (Adornes Estate – Jerusalem Chapel)

The Adornes domain consists of the mansion of the rich Adornes family of merchants, the 15th-century Jerusalem Chapel (built by this family) and a series of adjacent almshouses. In the multimedia museum, you step back in time to explore the life of Anselm Adornes and the Burgundian world in which he lived.

OPEN > 1/10 to 31/3: Monday to Saturday, 10.00 a.m.-5.00 p.m.; 1/4 to 30/9: Monday to Friday, 10.00 a.m.-5.00 p.m. and Saturday, 10.00 a.m.-6.00 p.m.

ADDITIONAL CLOSING DATES >
All (Belgian) public holidays

PRICE > €8; 65+: €6; youngsters aged 7 to 25: €4; children under 7: free; family discount: free entrance from the third child onwards

INFO > Peperstraat 3A, tel. +32 (0)50 33 88 83, www.adornes.org

02 Archeologiemuseum (Archaeological Museum)

This museum presents the unwritten history of Bruges. Its motto: feel your past beneath your feet. Discover the history of the city through different kinds of search and hands-on activities. A fascinating mix of archaeological finds, riddles, replicas and reconstructions shed light on daily life in times gone by, from the home to the workplace and from birth till death.

OPEN > Tuesday to Sunday, 9.30 a.m.-12.30 p.m. and 1.30 p.m.-5.00 p.m. (open on Easter Monday and Whit Monday; 24/12 and 31/12 until 4.00 p.m.); last admission: 30 min. before closing time

ADDITIONAL CLOSING DATES >
1/1, 30/5 (1.00 p.m.-5.00 p.m.) and 25/12

PRICE > €4; 65+ and youngsters aged 18 to 25: €3; children under 18: free

INFO > Mariastraat 36A, tel. +32 (0)50 44 87 43, www.museabrugge.be

03 Arentshuis

On the upper floor of this elegant city mansion with its picturesque garden (16th to 19th century) the oeuvre of the versatile British artist Frank Brangwyn (1867-1956) is on display. Brangwyn was both a graphic artist and a painter, as well as a designer of carpets, furniture and ceramics. The ground floor is the setting for temporary plastic art exhibitions.

OPEN > Tuesday to Sunday, 9.30 a.m.-5.00 p.m. (open on Easter Monday and Whit Monday; 24/12 and 31/12 until 4.00 p.m.); last admission: 30 min. before closing time
ADDITIONAL CLOSING DATES > 1/1, 30/5 (1.00 p.m.-5.00 p.m.) and 25/12
PRICE > €6; 65+ and youngsters aged 18 to 25: €5; children under 18: free; combination ticket with Groeninge Museum possible *(see pages 63-64)*
INFO > Dijver 16, tel. +32 (0)50 44 87 43, www.museabrugge.be

01 Basiliek van het Heilig Bloed (Basilica of the Holy Blood)

The double church, dedicated to Our Lady and Saint Basil in the 12th century and a basilica since 1923, consists of a lower church that has maintained its Romanesque character and a neo-Gothic upper church, in which the relic of the Holy Blood is preserved. The treasury, with numerous valuable works of art, is also worth a visit.
OPEN > Daily, 9.30 a.m.-12.30 p.m. and 2.00 p.m.-5.30 p.m.; last admission: 15 min. before closing time. Veneration of the relic: daily, 11.30 a.m.-12.00 p.m. and 2.00 p.m.-4.00 p.m.
ADDITIONAL CLOSING DATE > 1/1
PRICE > Double church: free; treasury: €2.50; children under 13: free
INFO > Burg 13, tel. +32 (0)50 33 67 92, www.holyblood.com

02 02 04 Begijnhof (Beguinage)

The 'Princely Beguinage Ten Wijngaarde' with its white-coloured house fronts and tranquil convent garden was founded in 1245. This little piece of world heritage was once the home of the beguines, emancipated lay-women who nevertheless led a pious and celibate life. Today the beguinage is inhabited by nuns of the Order of St. Benedict and several Bruges women who have decided to remain unmarried. In the Beguine's house, you can still get a good idea of what day-to-day life was like in the 17th century.
OPEN > Beguine's house: daily, 10.00 a.m.-5.00 p.m.; Beguinage: daily, 6.30 a.m.-6.30 p.m.
PRICE > Beguine's house: €2; 65+: €1.50; students (on display of a valid

student card) and children aged 8 to 12: €1. Beguinage: free
INFO > Begijnhof 24-28-30, tel. +32 (0)50 33 00 11, www.monasteria.org

05 09 Belfort (Belfry)

The most important of Bruges' towers stands 83 metres tall. It houses, amongst other things, a carillon. In the reception area, visitors can discover all kinds of interesting information about the history and working of this unique world heritage protected belfry. Those who take on the challenge of climbing the tower can pause for a breather on the way up in the old treasury and also at the level of the impressive clock or in the carillonneur's chamber. Finally, after a tiring 366 steps, your efforts will be rewarded with a breathtaking and unforgettable panoramic view of Bruges and its surroundings.

OPEN > Daily, 9.30 a.m.-6.00 p.m. (24/12 and 31/12 until 4.00 p.m.); last admission: 1 hour before closing time. For safety reasons, only a limited number of people will be allowed to visit the tower at the same time. Reservations are not possible. Please consider a certain waiting period.
ADDITIONAL CLOSING DATES >
1/1, 30/5 (1.00 p.m.-6.00 p.m.) and 25/12
PRICE > €12; 65+ and youngsters aged 6 to 25: €10; children under 6: free
INFO > Markt 7, tel. +32 (0)50 44 87 43, www.museabrugge.be

Bezoekerscentrum Lissewege – Heiligenmuseum (Visitors Centre Lissewege – Saints' Museum)

The Visitors' Centre tells the story of 'the white village', which dates back through more than a thousand years of history. In the Saints' Museum, you can admire a remarkable collection of more than 130 antique statues of patron saints.
OPEN > During the long weekend of 1 May (1/5 to 5/5), on weekends in May and June, during Ascension weekend

(30/5 to 2/6), during Whit weekend (8/6 to 10/6), 1/7 to 15/9 and in the last two weekends of September (21/9-22/9 and 28/9-29/9): 2.00 p.m.-5.30 p.m.
PRICE > Saints' Museum: €2; children under 12: €1
INFO > Oude Pastoriestraat 5, Lissewege, tel. +32 (0)495 38 70 95, www.lissewege.be

Boudewijn Seapark Bruges

In the Boudewijn Seapark you can enjoy the magical new dolphin show and watch the seals and sea lions perform the craziest tricks. But it is not only the sea mammals in this family park that will charm you, but also the twenty outdoor park attractions that offer guaranteed fun for young and old alike. Finally, *Bobo's Indoor* has ten great indoor attractions, and *Bobo's Aqua Splash* provides hours of wonderful water fun outdoors.
OPEN > During the period 6/4 to 29/9. During the Easter holidays (6/4 to 22/4) and 27/4 to 1/5: 10.00 a.m.-5.00 p.m.; in May and June: daily, except on Wednesday, 10.00 a.m.-5.00 p.m.; in July and August: daily, 10.00 a.m.-6.00 p.m.; September: Saturday and Sunday, 10.00 a.m.-6.00 p.m.; during autumn school holiday (26/10 to 3/11): 10.00 a.m.-5.00 p.m. Consult the website for details of opening and availability during the winter period.
PRICE > €26.50; 65+ and children taller than 1 metre and under 12 years old: €24.50; children between 85 cm and 99 cm: €9.50
INFO > Alfons De Baeckestraat 12, Sint-Michiels, tel. +32 (0)50 38 38 38, www.boudewijnseapark.be. Tickets at the amusement park entrance or at the i tourist office 't Zand (Concert Hall).

09 Brouwerij Bourgogne des Flandres (Brewery)

After an absence of 60 years, *Bourgogne des Flandres* is once again being brewed in Bruges. You can learn from the brewer himself how the beer is made, as well as tapping a digital glass in the interactive space. Or perhaps you can have a bottle of the delicious brew personalized with your photo? The kids can amuse themselves with a fun treasure hunt. If you are still feeling

thirsty after your visit, you can enjoy a glass of something pleasant on the romantic terrace overlooking the water.

OPEN > Tuesday to Sunday, 10.00 a.m.-6.00 p.m., but during Belgian school holidays, long weekends and public holidays also on Monday; last guided tour starts at 5.00 p.m.

ADDITIONAL CLOSING DATES >
1/1, 7/1 to 22/1 and 25/12

PRICE > Including one taster and an audio guide (available in 10 languages): €11; children aged 10 to 15: €5 (without taster); children under 10: free; family ticket (2 adults + 3 children max.): €28, including a drink for the adults

INFO > Kartuizerinnenstraat 6, tel. +32 (0)50 33 54 26, www.bourgognedesflandres.be

10 Brouwerij De Halve Maan (Brewery)

This authentic brewery in the centre of Bruges is a family business with a tradition stretching back through six generations to 1856. This is where the Bruges city beer – the *Brugse Zot* – is brewed: a strong-tasting, high-fermentation beer based on malt, hops and special yeast. In 2016, a unique underground beer pipeline, some 3 km long, was laid from the brewery to the bottling plant in the suburbs.

OPEN > Shop: daily, 10.00 a.m.-5.00 p.m. (Saturday until 6.00 p.m.). Guided tours: Sunday to Friday, every hour between 11.00 a.m. and 4.00 p.m., the last tour leaving at 4.00 p.m.; Saturday, between 11.00 a.m. 5 p.m. every hour, the last tour leaving at 5.00 p.m.; XL-tour with a tasting of three special beers: daily, at 2.15 p.m.

ADDITIONAL CLOSING DATES >
1/1 and 25/12

PRICE > Including taster: €12 (online €11); children aged 6 to 12: €6; children under 6: free; XL-Tour: €21

LANGUAGES > English, Dutch, French. XL-Tour: English, Dutch

INFO > Walplein 26, tel. +32 (0)50 44 42 22, www.halvemaan.be

12 Bruges Beer Experience

Discover in an interactive way everything you ever wanted to know about the raw ingredients of beer, the brewing process, food pairing, beer in Bruges, trappist and

abbey beers, etc. Children follow the Kids Tour, which tells the story of the Bruges Bear. Would you just like to sample some beers? The bar and its 16 different kinds of beer is open to everyone and has a great view over the Market Square.
OPEN > Daily, 10.00 a.m.-6.00 p.m.; last admission: 1 hour before closing time (bar and shop are open until 6.30 p.m.)
ADDITIONAL CLOSING DATES >
1/1 and 25/12
PRICE > Including iPad Mini with headphones (available in 11 languages): €16 (with 3 beer samples) or €10 (without beer samples); children aged 5 to 12: €6; family ticket (max. 2 adults + 3 children): €36 (with beer samples) or €24 (without beer samples)
INFO > Breidelstraat 3 (top floor former Post Office), tel. +32 (0)50 69 92 29 or +32 (0)496 76 45 54, www.mybeerexperience.com

03 07 13 Brugse Vrije (Liberty of Bruges)

From this mansion, the Liberty of Bruges (the countryside in a wide area around the city) was once governed. The building functioned as a court of justice between 1795 and 1984. Today, the City Archive (amongst other things) is housed here. They safeguard Bruges' written memory. The premises also boast an old assize court and a renaissance hall with a monumental 16th-century timber, marble and alabaster fireplace made by Lanceloot Blondeel.
OPEN > Daily, 9.30 a.m.- 5.00 p.m. (24/12 and 31/12 until 4.00 p.m.); last admission: 30 min. before closing time
ADDITIONAL CLOSING DATES >
1/1, 30/5 (1.00 p.m.-5.00 p.m.) and 25/12
PRICE > Including City Hall: €6; 65+ and youngsters aged 18 to 25: €5; children under 18: free. Tickets are sold in the City Hall.
APP > You can visit the Liberty of Bruges with the Xplore Bruges app (www.xplorebruges.be).
INFO > Burg 11A, tel. +32 (0)50 44 87 43, www.museabrugge.be

14 Choco-Story (Chocolate Museum)

The museum dips its visitors in the history of cocoa and chocolate. From the Maya and the Spanish conquistadores to the chocolate connoisseurs of today. Children can explore the museum via a fun chocolate search game. Chocolates are made by hand and sampled on the premises. A 5-minute walk brings you to Vlamingstraat 31, where you will find the Choco-Jungle Bar, which is also part of the museum.
OPEN > Daily, 10.00 a.m.-5.00 p.m. (1/7 to 31/8, until 6.00 p.m.); last admission: 45 min. before closing time

ADDITIONAL CLOSING DATES > 1/1, 7/1 to 11/1 and 25/12
PRICE > €9.50; 65+ and students (on display of a valid student card): €7.50; children aged 6 to 11: €5.50; children under 6: free; several combination tickets possible *(see page 75)*
LANGUAGES > App with audio guide available in German, Spanish, Italian, Japanese. There are info-boards in Dutch, French and English.
INFO > Wijnzakstraat 2, tel. +32 (0)50 61 22 37, www.choco-story.be

17 Concertgebouw Circuit

An original experience trail takes you on an expedition through the modern Concert Hall. Learn how the concert hall works, be impressed by its famous acoustics, thrill to its contemporary art collection or perhaps even get started with a little sound art yourself!

The icing on the cake is the rooftop terrace on the seventh floor, rewarding you with a breathtaking panoramic view over the city.
OPEN > Wednesday to Saturday, 2.00 p.m.-6.00 p.m.; Sunday, 10.00 a.m.-2.00 p.m.; last admission: 30 min. before closing time. Guided tours (prior reservation necessary): Wednesday to Saturday at 3.00 p.m.
ADDITIONAL CLOSING DATES > 1/1 and 25/12. Sometimes (exceptionally) not open to the public; please check the website before planning your visit.
PRICE > €8; youngsters aged 6 to 26: €4; children younger than 6: free; guided tour: no additional charge
LANGUAGES > English, Dutch, French
APP > Use the app Xplore Bruges (www.xplorebruges.be) and go on a musical journey through Bruges' past to discover the soundtrack of a medieval city (tip: make sure you have earbuds or headphones with you).
INFO > 't Zand 34, tel. +32 (0)50 47 69 99, www.concertgebouwcircuit.be

Cozmix – Volkssterrenwacht (Public Observatory) Beisbroek

Admire the beauty of the sun, moon and planets in glorious closeup, thanks to a powerful telescope. In the planetarium more than seven thousand stars are projected onto the interior of the dome. Spectacular video images take you on a journey through the mysteries of the universe. The artistic planet-pathway (with sculptures by Jef Claerhout) will

complete your voyage of discovery into outer space.

OPEN > Wednesday and Sunday, 2.30 p.m.-6.00 p.m.; Friday, 8.00 p.m.-10.00 p.m. Planetarium shows on Wednesday and Sunday at 3.00 p.m. and 4.30 p.m. and on Friday at 8.30 p.m. Extended opening hours and extra planetarium shows during Belgian school holidays; please consult the website.

ADDITIONAL CLOSING DATES > 1/1 and 25/12

PRICE > €6; youngsters aged 4 to 17: €5

LANGUAGES > Shows in languages other than Dutch on Wednesday at 4.30 p.m.: first and third weeks of the month in French, second, fourth and fifth weeks in English

INFO > Zeeweg 96, Sint-Andries, tel. +32 (0)50 39 05 66, www.cozmix.be

18 Diamantmuseum Brugge (Bruges Diamond Museum)

Did you know that the technique of cutting diamonds was first applied in Bruges almost 550 years ago? This is just one of the many fascinating stories you will hear in the Bruges Diamond Museum. You can learn even more diamond secrets during the diamond cutting show, when you will actually get to see how the gems are cut.

OPEN > Daily, 10.30 a.m.-5.30 p.m. Diamond cutting show: multiple shows daily; the programme can be consulted on-site, over the phone or online.

ADDITIONAL CLOSING DATES > 1/1, 7/1 to 18/1 and 25/12

PRICE > Including cutting demonstration: €9.50; 65+, students (on display of a valid student card) and children aged 6 to 12: €8.50; children under 6: free; family ticket (2 adults + 2 children): €30; a combination ticket is possible *(see page 75)*

LANGUAGES > Diamond cutting show in English, French, Dutch

INFO > Katelijnestraat 43, tel. +32 (0)50 34 20 56, www.diamondmuseum.be

20 Foltermuseum De Oude Steen (Torture Museum)

In the beautifully renovated – and probably oldest stone – building in Bruges, you can discover a remarkable and spine-chilling collection of instruments of torture and learn about the history of law, order and justice in the city. Guaranteed to make you reflect on the complex medieval relationship be-

tween good and evil, and how the justice of the day continuously balanced on the border between violence and righteousness.
OPEN > Daily, 10.30 a.m.-6.30 p.m. (1/7 to 31/8, until 9.00 p.m.)
PRICE > €8; 60+: €7; students: €6; children under 11: free; family ticket (2 adults + 3 children under 16): €20
INFO > Wollestraat 29, tel. +32 (0)50 73 41 34, www.torturemuseum.be

08 21 Frietmuseum (Belgian Fries Museum)

This didactical museum sketches the history of the potato, Belgian fries and the various sauces and dressings that accompany this most delicious and most famous of Belgian comestibles. The museum is housed in the Saaihalle, one of Bruges' most attractive buildings. Show your entrance ticket and enjoy a €0.40 discount on a portion of fries.
OPEN > Daily, 10.00 a.m.-5.00 p.m.; last admission: 45 min. before closing time
ADDITIONAL CLOSING DATES > 1/1, 7/1 to 11/1 and 25/12
PRICE > €7; 65+ and students (on display of a valid student card): €6; children aged 6 to 11: €5; children

under 6: free; several combination tickets possible *(see page 75)*
LANGUAGES > App with audio guide available in English, Dutch, French, German, Spanish, Italian
INFO > Vlamingstraat 33, tel. +32 (0)50 34 01 50, www.frietmuseum.be

07 22 Gentpoort (Gate of Ghent)

The Gate of Ghent is one of four remaining medieval city gates. An entrance for foreigners, a border with the outside world for the townspeople of Bruges. The gate was a part of the city's defences as well as a passageway for the movement of produce and merchandise. The Gate of Ghent is at its most beautiful in the evening, when it is quite literally in the spotlight.
OPEN > Tuesday to Sunday, 9.30 a.m.-12.30 p.m. and 1.30 p.m.-5.00 p.m. (open

on Easter Monday and Whit Monday; 24/12 and 31/12 until 4.00 p.m.); last admission: 30 min. before closing time
ADDITIONAL CLOSING DATES > 1/1, 30/5 (1.00 p.m.-5 p.m.) and 25/12
PRICE > €4; 65+ and youngsters aged 18 to 25: €3; children under 18: free
INFO > Gentpoortvest, tel. +32 (0)50 44 87 43, www.museabrugge.be

23 Gezellemuseum (Gezelle Museum)

This literary and biographical museum about the life of Guido Gezelle (1830-1899), one of Flanders' most famous poets, was established in the house where he was born, situated in a peaceful working-class district of the city. In addition to displays about his life and works, there are also temporary presentations about (literary) art. Behind the house there is a romantic garden,

with Jan Fabre's *The Man Who Gives a Light* as the main attraction.
OPEN > Tuesday to Sunday, 9.30 a.m.-12.30 p.m. and 1.30 p.m.-5.00 p.m. (open on Easter Monday and Whit Monday; 24/12 and 31/12 until 4.00 p.m.); last admission: 30 min. before closing time
ADDITIONAL CLOSING DATES > 1/1, 30/5 (1.00 p.m.-5.00 p.m.) and 25/12
PRICE > €4; 65+ and youngsters aged 18 to 25: €3; children under 18: free
INFO > Rolweg 64, tel. +32 (0)50 44 87 43, www.museabrugge.be

24 Groeningemuseum (Groeninge Museum)

The Groeninge Museum provides a varied overview of the history of Belgian visual art, with the world-renowned Flemish primitives as a highlight. In this museum you can see, amongst other masterpieces, *Madonna with Canon Joris Van der Paele* by Jan van Eyck and the *Moreel Triptych* by Hans Memling. You will also marvel at the top 18th and 19th-century neoclassical pieces, masterpieces of Flemish Expressionism and post-war modern art.
OPEN > Tuesday to Sunday, 9.30 a.m.-

5.00 p.m. (open on Easter Monday and Whit Monday; 24/12 and 31/12 until 4.00 p.m.); last admission: 30 min. before closing time
ADDITIONAL CLOSING DATES > 1/1, 30/5 (1.00 p.m.-5.00 p.m.) and 25/12
PRICE > Including Arentshuis: €12; 65+ and youngsters aged 18 to 25: €10; children under 18: free; a combination ticket is possible *(see page 75)*
INFO > Dijver 12, tel. +32 (0)50 44 87 43, www.museabrugge.be

Reopening in 2019

25 Gruuthuse-museum (Gruuthuse Museum)

This year, one of Bruges' finest monuments reopens its doors following major renovation. The city palace of the lords of Gruuthuse introduces you to many stories from the city's fascinating past. This rich history is explored through a fine collection of tapestries, paintings, archive documents, lace and silverware.
OPEN > As of spring 2019: Tuesday to Sunday, 9.30 a.m.-5.00 p.m. (open on Whit Monday; 24/12 and 31/12 until 4.00 p.m.); last admission: 30 min. before closing time
ADDITIONAL CLOSING DATES > 30/5 (1.00 p.m.-5.00 p.m.) and 25/12
PRICE > €12; 65+ and youngsters aged 18 to 25: €10; children under 18: free; a combination ticket is possible *(see page 75)*
LANGUAGES > Free audio guide available in 6 languages
INFO > Dijver 17C, tel. +32 (0)50 44 87 43, www.museabrugge.be

07 Heilige Magdalenakerk (St. Magdalene's Church)

The St. Magdalene's Church, built in the mid-19th century, was one of the earliest

neo-Gothic churches on the European mainland. This style of architecture, first made popular in England, was brought to Bruges by British immigrants. That is how the neo-Gothic appeared in the streets of Bruges quite early. Inside the church you can make your acquaintance with YOT, an organization that explores the meaning of the Christian tradition in modern society.

OPEN > 1/1 to 31/3: Friday to Monday, 2.00 p.m.-5.00 p.m.; 1/4 to 30/9: daily, 11.00 a.m.-6.00 p.m.; 1/10 to 31/12: daily, 1.00 p.m.-6.00 p.m.
The church is not open for visitors during liturgical services.

ADDITIONAL CLOSING DATES >
1/1, 24/12, 25/12 and 31/12

PRICE > Free

INFO > Corner Stalijzerstraat and Schaarstraat, tel. +32 (0)50 33 68 18, www.yot.be

26

Historium Bruges

In the Historium, you quite literally step back in time. In different ways you will be able to learn about the vibrant city of Bruges during the Golden Century. *Historium Story* tells the love story of Jan van Eyck's apprentice, Jacob. After that, you can discover more about Bruges in the Middle Ages in the *Historium Exhibition*. *Historium Virtual Reality* takes you back to the year 1435, allowing you to sail virtually into the old city port, where you will fly past the Water Halls and the Saint Donatian's Church, both of which have long since disappeared. The *Historium Tower* takes you up the 30-metre high Neo-Gothic tower for a stunning view over the Markt.

OPEN > Daily, 10.00 a.m.-6.00 p.m.; last admission: 1 hour before closing time

PRICE > All Historium tickets include an audio guide (available in 10 languages): Explorer (Story + Exhibition): €14; students: €10; children aged 3 to 12: €7.50; Time Traveller (Story + Exhibition + Virtual Reality): €17.50; Thirsty Time Traveller (same as Time Traveller + drink of your choice in the Duvelorium): €19.50; Virtual Reality: €6; Tower: €6;

a combination ticket is possible
(see page 75)
INFO > Markt 1, tel. +32 (0)50 27 03 11, www.historium.be

29
Kantcentrum (Lace Centre)

The Lace Centre has been housed in the renovated old lace school of the Sisters of the Immaculate Conception. The story of Bruges lace is told in the Lace Museum on the ground floor. Multimedia installations and testimonies from international lace experts help to explain the various different types of lace and their geographical origin, and focus on the lace industry and lace education in Bruges. Demonstrations and various courses are organized in the lace workshop on the second floor.

OPEN > Monday to Saturday, 9.30 a.m.-5.00 p.m.; last admission: 30 min.before closing time. Demonstrations: Monday to Saturday, 2.00 p.m.-5.00 p.m.

ADDITIONAL CLOSING DATES >
All (Belgian) public holidays

PRICE > €6; 65+ and youngsters aged 12 to 26: €5; children under 12: free; a combination ticket is possible (see page 75)

INFO > Balstraat 16, tel. +32 (0)50 33 00 72, www.kantcentrum.eu

30
Lumina Domestica (Lamp Museum)

The museum contains the world's largest collection of lamps and lights. More than six thousand antiques tell the complete story of interior lighting, from the torch and paraffin lamp to the light bulb and LED. The small detour into the world of luminous animals and plants is particularly interesting. In this way you can discover, for example, the light mysteries of the glow-worm, the lantern fish and the small Chinese lantern.

OPEN > Daily, 10.00 a.m.-5.00 p.m. (1/7 to 31/8, until 6.00 p.m.); last admission: 45 min. before closing time

ADDITIONAL CLOSING DATES >
1/1, 7/1 to 11/1 and 25/12

PRICE > €7; 65+ and students (on display of a valid student card): €6; children aged 6 to 11: €5; children under 6: free; several combination tickets possible (see page 75)

INFO > Wijnzakstraat 2, tel. +32 (0)50 61 22 37, www.luminadomestica.be

Onze-Lieve-Vrouw-Bezoekingkerk Lissewege (Church of Our Lady of Visitation)

The 13th-century brick Church of Our Lady of Visitation is a textbook example of 'coastal Gothic'. A lack of money meant that the tower was never finished, which accounts for its rather 'blunt' appearance. Its interior has a miraculous statue of the Virgin Mary (1625), an exceptional organ case and a beautifully sculptured rood loft and pulpit (1652).

OPEN > 1/5 to 30/9: daily, 9.00 a.m.-6.00 p.m.; 1/10 to 30/4: daily, 10.00 a.m.-4.00 p.m.

PRICE > Free

INFO > Onder de Toren, Lissewege, tel. +32 (0)50 54 45 44, www.lissewege.be

♿ 15 32

Onze-Lieve-Vrouwekerk (Church of Our Lady)

The 115.5-metre high brick tower of the Church of Our Lady is a perfect illustration of the craftsmanship of Bruges' artisans. The church displays a valuable art collection: Michelangelo's world-famous *Madonna and Child*, countless paintings, 13th-century painted sepulchres and the tombs of Mary of Burgundy and Charles the Bold. The choir was renovated in 2015 and the remarkable church interior can now once again be admired in all its splendour.

OPEN > Monday to Saturday, 9.30 a.m.-5.00 p.m.; Sunday and Holy Days, 1.30 p.m.-5.00 p.m.; last admission: 30 min. before closing time. The church and the museum are not open to visitors during nuptial and funeral masses. Useful to know: from January to the end of March 2019 (subject to confirmation), restoration work will be carried out on the altar of the *Madonna and Child*.

ADDITIONAL CLOSING DATES > Museum: 1/1, 30/5 and 25/12

PRICE > Church: free. Museum: €6; 65+ and youngsters aged 18 to 25: €5; children under 18: free. There is a reduced entrance fee during the restoration work.

INFO > Mariastraat, tel. +32 (0)50 44 87 43, www.museabrugge.be

16 33 Onze-Lieve-Vrouw-ter-Potterie (Our Lady of the Pottery)

This hospital dates back to the 13th century, when nuns took on the care of pilgrims, travellers and the sick. In the

15th century, it evolved towards a more modern type of home for the elderly. The hospital wards with their valuable collection of works of art, monastic and religious relics and a range of objects used in nursing have been converted into a museum. The Gothic church with its baroque interior can also be visited.

OPEN > Tuesday to Sunday, 9.30 a.m.-12.30 p.m. and 1.30 p.m.-5.00 p.m. (open on Easter Monday and Whit Monday; 24/12 and 31/12 until 4.00 p.m.); last admission: 30 min. before closing time

ADDITIONAL CLOSING DATES >
1/1, 30/5 (1.00 p.m.-5.00 p.m.) and 25/12

PRICE > Church: free. Museum: €6; 65+ and youngsters aged 18 to 25: €5; children under 18: free

INFO > Potterierei 79B, tel. +32 (0)50 44 87 43, www.museabrugge.be

17 Onze-Lieve-Vrouw-van-Blindekenskapel (Chapel of our Lady of the Blind)

The original wooden Chapel of Our Lady of Blindekens was erected in 1305 as an expression of gratitude to Our Lady after the Battle of Mons-en-Pévèle (1304). The current chapel dates from 1651. In order to fulfil the 'Bruges promise', made on the field of battle, the Blindekens procession has paraded through the streets of the city on 15th August every year since 1305. As part of the procession, the women of Bruges donate a candle (of 18 kilograms) to the Church of Onze-Lieve-Vrouw-ter-Potterie.

OPEN > Daily, 9.00 a.m.-6.00 p.m.

PRICE > Free

INFO > Kreupelenstraat 8, tel. +32 (0)50 32 76 60 or +32 (0)50 33 68 41, www.brugsebelofte.be

35 Museum-Gallery Xpo Salvador Dalí

In the Cloth Halls, you can admire a fantastic collection of world-famous graphics and statues by the great artist Dalí. They are all authentic works of art that are described in the *Catalogues Raisonnés*, which details Salvador Dalí's oeuvre. The collection is presented in a sensational *Daliesque* décor of mirrors, gold and shocking pink.

OPEN > Daily, 10.00 a.m.-6.00 p.m. (24/12 and 31/12, until 3.30 p.m.)

ADDITIONAL CLOSING DATES >
1/1 and 25/12

PRICE > €10; 65+, students (on display of a valid student card) and youngsters

aged 13 to 18: €8; children under 13: free
LANUAGES > Audio guide available in 3 languages: €2
INFO > Markt 7, tel. +32 (0)50 33 83 44, www.dali-interart.be

Seafront Zeebrugge

There is lots to do and discover in the buildings of the Old Fish Market: as well as shops, restaurants and cafes, you will also find the Seafront theme park. Learn about coastal tourism past and present, explore the fascinating world of fish and fishing, and let yourself by catapulted back in time to the era of the hellish World Wars. The West-Hinder lightship, which once guided ships safely at sea, is now permanently moored alongside the quay as a reminder of a rich maritime heritage.
OPEN > Seafront continues to develop. Among other things, there is a varied program of (temporary) exhibitions on themes relating to the sea. Make sure you check the website before your visit for the most up-to-date information.
PRICE > From €9.50
INFO > Vismijnstraat 7, Zeebrugge, tel. +32 (0)50 55 14 15, www.seafront.be

19 Sint-Annakerk (St. Anne's Church)

This simple Gothic single-nave church, built in the 17th century, surprises with the opulence of its rich Baroque interior – the result of donations by wealthy local patrons. Admire the intricacy of the marble rood-screen, the rich wooden panelling with inset confessional booths, the canvases of Jan Garemijn and the largest single painting in all Bruges.
OPEN > 1/1 to 31/3: Friday to Monday, 2.00 p.m.-5.00 p.m.; 1/4 to 30/9: daily, 11.00 a.m.-6.00 p.m.; 1/10 to 31/12: daily, 1.00 p.m.-6.00 p.m. The church is not open to visitors during liturgical services.
ADDITIONAL CLOSING DATES > 1/1, 24/12, 25/12 and 31/12
PRICE > Free
INFO > Sint-Annaplein, tel. +32 (0)50 34 87 05, www.sintdonatianusbrugge.be

20 Sint-Gilliskerk (St. Giles' Church)

In this church, the only one in the city centre with a tower clock, many of the great Bruges artists have been buried. These include Hans Memling, Lanceloot Blondeel and Pieter Pourbus. The church originally dates from the

13th century, but was extensively rebuilt in the 15th century. The exterior is a fine example of the robust Brick Gothic style, while the interior has a more refined 19th-century neo-Gothic look.
OPEN > 1/1 to 31/3: Friday to Monday, 2.00 p.m.-5.00 p.m.; 1/4 to 30/9: daily, 11.00 a.m.- 6.00 p.m.; 1/10 to 31/12: daily, 1.00 p.m.-6.00 p.m. The church is not open to visitors during religious services.
ADDITIONAL CLOSING DATES >
1/1, 24/12, 25/12 and 31/12
PRICE > Free
INFO > Baliestraat 2, tel. +32 (0)50 34 87 05, www.sintdonatianusbrugge.be

22 Sint-Jakobskerk (St. James's Church)

In the second quarter of the 13th century, the modest St. James's Chapel was elevated to the status of a parish church. During the 15th century, this simple house of prayer was extended to its current size. The church is now famous for its rich collection of art treasures, donated by wealthy local people living nearby, and for its fine examples of funerary art.
OPEN > 1/1 to 31/3: Friday to Monday, 2.00 p.m.-5.00 p.m.; 1/4 to 30/9: daily,

11.00 a.m.-6.00 p.m.; 1/10 to 31/12: daily, 1.00 p.m.-6.00 p.m. The church is not open to visitors during religious services.
ADDITIONAL CLOSING DATES >
1/1, 24/12, 25/12 and 31/12
PRICE > Free
APP > Discover 15 masterpieces in the church via the Xplore Bruges app (www.xplorebruges.be).
INFO > Sint-Jakobsplein, tel. +32 (0)50 33 68 41, www.sintdonatianusbrugge.be

36 Sint-Janshospitaal (Saint John's Hospital)

Saint John's Hospital has an eight hundred-year-old history of caring for pilgrims, travellers, the poor and the sick. Visit the medieval wards, as well as the church and the chapel, and marvel at the impressive collection of archives, art works, medical instruments and six

paintings by Hans Memling. Also worth a visit: the Diksmuide attic, the old dormitory, the adjoining custodian's room and the pharmacy.

OPEN > Museum and pharmacy: Tuesday to Sunday, 9.30 a.m.-5.00 p.m. (both open on Easter Monday and Whit Monday; 24/12 and 31/12 until 4.00 p.m.); last admission: 30 min. before closing time

ADDITIONAL CLOSING DATES >
1/1, 30/5 (1.00 p.m.-5.00 p.m.) and 25/12

PRICE > Including visit to the pharmacy: €12; 65+ and youngsters aged 18 to 25: €10; children under 18: free

APP > You can learn more about the six works of Hans Memling via the Xplore Bruges app (www.xplorebruges.be).

INFO > Mariastraat 38, tel. +32 (0)50 44 87 43, www.museabrugge.be

37 Sint-Janshuismolen (Mill)

Windmills have graced Bruges' ramparts ever since the construction of the outer city wall at the end of the 13th century. Today four specimens are left on Kruisvest. The Sint-Janshuis Mill, built in 1770 and still occupying its original site, is the only mill still grinding flour and the only mill open to visitors.

OPEN > 1/4 to 30/9: Tuesday to Sunday, 9.30 a.m.-12.30 p.m. and 1.30 p.m.-5.00 p.m. (open on Easter Monday and Whit Monday); last admission: 30 min. before closing time

ADDITIONAL CLOSING DATE > 30/5 (1.00 p.m.-5.00 p.m.)
PRICE > €4; 65+ and youngsters aged 18 to 25: €3; children under 18: free
INFO > Kruisvest, tel. +32 (0)50 44 87 43, www.museabrugge.be

23 Sint-Salvatorskathedraal (Saint Saviour's Cathedral)

Bruges' oldest parish church (12th-15th century) has amongst its treasures a rood loft with an organ, medieval tombs, Brussels tapestries and a rich collection of Flemish paintings (14th-18th century). The treasure-chamber displays, amongst others, paintings by Dieric Bouts, Hugo van der Goes and other Flemish primitives.
OPEN > Cathedral: Monday to Friday, 10.00 a.m.-1.00 p.m. and 2.00 p.m.-5.30 p.m.; Saturday, 10.00 a.m.-1.00 p.m. and 2.00 p.m.-3.30 p.m.; Sunday, 11.30 a.m.-12.00 p.m. and 2.00 p.m.-5.00 p.m. The cathedral is not open to visitors during liturgical services. Treasury: daily (except Saturday), 2.00 p.m.- 5.00 p.m.
ADDITIONAL CLOSING DATES > Cathedral (afternoon) and treasury (all day): 1/1, 30/5, 24/12 and 25/12
PRICE > Cathedral and Treasury: free
INFO > Steenstraat, tel. +32 (0)50 33 61 88, www.sintsalvator.be

24 Sint-Walburgakerk (St. Walburga's Church)

In 1619, a Bruges lay brother, Pieter Huyssens, was commissioned to build a prestigious church that expressed the values and beliefs of the Jesuits. The result was the St. Walburga's Church, which is the most richly decorated church in pure Baroque style in Bruges. Admire its dynamic facade,

its many interior architectural details and the elaborately decorated church furniture.

OPEN > 1/1 to 31/3: Friday to Monday, 2.00 p.m.-5.00 p.m.; 1/4 to 30/9: daily, 11.00 a.m.-6.00 p.m.; 1/10 to 31/12: daily, 1.00 p.m.-6.00 p.m.

ADDITIONAL CLOSING DATES > 1/1, 24/12, 25/12 and 31/12

PRICE > Free

INFO > Sint-Maartensplein, tel. +32 (0)50 34 87 05, www.sintdonatianusbrugge.be

08 40

Stadhuis (City Hall)

Bruges' City Hall (1376-1420) is one of the oldest in the Low Countries. It is from here that the city has been governed for more than 600 years. An absolute masterpiece is the Gothic Hall, with its late 19th-century murals and polychrome vault. In the historic chamber next door, original documents and artefacts are used to evoke the history of the city's administration through the centuries. On the ground floor, the structural development of the Burg square and the City Hall is illustrated.

OPEN > Daily, 9.30 a.m.-5.00 p.m. (24/12 and 31/12 until 4.00 p.m.); last admission: 30 min. before closing time. The Gothic Hall and the historic chamber are not open to visitors during weddings.

ADDITIONAL CLOSING DATES > 1/1, 30/5 (1.00 p.m.-5.00 p.m.) and 25/12

PRICE > Including visit of Liberty of Bruges: €6; 65+ and youngsters aged 18 to 25: €5; children under 18: free

APP > Visit the City Hall with the free app Xplore Bruges (www.xplorebruges.be).

LANGUAGES > Free audio guide available in 5 languages

INFO > Burg 12, tel. +32 (0)50 44 87 43, www.museabrugge.be

42 Volkskundemuseum (Museum of Folk Life)

These renovated 17th century almshouses accommodate, amongst other things, a classroom, a millinery, a pharmacy, a confectionery shop and a grocery shop. On the upper floor, you can experience first-hand what it was like to be a child during the period 1930-1960. You can relax in the museum inn, 'De Zwarte Kat' (The Black Cat) or in the garden, where you can try out traditional folk and children's games on the terrace.

OPEN > Museum and inn: Tuesday to Sunday, 9.30 a.m.-5.00 p.m. (open on Easter Monday and Whit Monday; 24/12 and 31/12 until 4.00 p.m.); last admission: 30 min. before closing time

ADDITIONAL CLOSING DATES > 1/1, 30/5 (1.00 p.m.-5.00 p.m.) and 25/12

PRICE > €6; 65+ and youngsters aged 18 to 25: €5; children under 18: free; a combination ticket is possible *(see page 75)*

INFO > Balstraat 43, tel. +32 (0)50 44 87 43, www.museabrugge.be

04 43 Xpo Center Bruges

On the historic Old Saint John site you can visit Expo Picasso, a permanent exhibition with 300 graphic works by the Spanish master Pablo Picasso and a hundred or so authentic works by the American artist Andy Warhol. In addition to these permanent exhibitions, the 19th century infirmary wards are also the setting each year for a variety of fascinating temporary expositions. This year you can visit *Mummies in Bruges – Secrets of Ancient Egypt* *(Read more on page 78)*.

OPEN > All exhibitions: daily, 10.00 a.m.-6.00 p.m.

ADDITIONAL CLOSING DATES > 1/1, 7/1 to 1/2 and 25/12

PRICE > Picasso: €10; 65+ and youngsters aged 6 to 18: €8. Picasso and Warhol: €12; 65+ and youngsters aged 6 to 18: €10. Mummies in Bruges: €14; 65+ and youngsters aged 6 to 18: €12. All-in ticket: €17.50; 65+ and youngsters aged 6 to 18: €15.50. Children under 6: free

INFO > Site Oud Sint-Jan, Mariastraat 38, tel. +32 (0)50 47 61 00, www.xpo-center-bruges.be

MAKE THE MOST OF IT!

» Musea Brugge Card

With the Musea Brugge Card you can visit the different Musea Brugge locations (www.museabrugge.be) as often as you like for just €28. Youngsters aged 18 to 25 pay just €22. The pass is valid for three consecutive days and can be purchased at all Musea Brugge locations (except for the Liberty of Bruges and the Sint-Janshuis Mill), at the i Markt (Historium) and at the i 't Zand (Concert Hall).

» Discount cards with your stay

Enjoy a discount on the admission fees to various museums, attractions and other sites of interest using the free Discover Bruges card that you get whenever you stay in one of the hotels affiliated with Hotels Regio Bruges vzw (www.discoverbruges.com) or the free Bruges Advantage City Card that you get whenever you spend at least two nights at one of the B&B's affiliated to the Gilde der Brugse Gastenverblijven vzw (www.brugge-bedandbreakfast.com).

» Combiticket Gruuthuse/Church of Our Lady (available from spring 2019 in the reception pavilion of the Gruuthuse Museum)

Pay a visit to the recently renovated Gruuthuse Museum, one of Bruges' finest monuments, which reopens its doors this spring. And while you are there, why not also pop in to the adjacent – and highly impressive – Church of Our Lady, with its 115.5-metre high brick tower and its rich art collection. This combination ticket costs €14.

» Combination ticket Historium/Groeninge Museum

Experience the golden century of Bruges in the Historium, with the painting of *Madonna with Canon Joris van der Paele* by Jan van Eyck as your leitmotif. Then see the masterpiece itself in the Groeninge Museum, along with the great works of many others of the so-called Flemish primitives. This €22 combination ticket is only available in the Historium.

» Combination ticket Choco-Story/Diamond Museum

Combine a tasty visit to Choco-Story with a dazzling look at the Diamond Museum. This combination ticket costs €17 (including diamond-cutting demonstration). For sale at the above-mentioned museums.

» Combination ticket Choco-Story/Lumina Domestica/Belgian Fries Museum

Visit these three museums at reduced rates.

- Combination ticket Choco-Story/Lumina Domestica: €11.50; 65+ and students: €9.50; children aged 6 to 11: €7.50; children under 6: free
- Combination ticket Choco-Story/Belgian Fries Museum: €14.50; 65+ and students: €11.50; children aged 6 to 11: €8.50; children under 6: free
- Combination ticket (3 museums): €16.50; 65+ and students: €13.50; children aged 6 to 11: €10.50; children under 6: free. These combination tickets are for sale at the above-mentioned museums and at the i tourist office 't Zand (Concert Hall).

» Combination ticket Lace Centre/Museum of Folk Life

The Lace Centre, displaying lacework from the Musea Brugge collection, is a great 'add-on' to your visit to the Museum of Folk Life, where, amongst other things, you can have a look inside a traditional tailor's shop. Combination ticket: €10, on sale in both museums.

Culture and events

Concertgebouw

The city's high-quality cultural life is flourishing like never before. Devotees of modern architecture stand in awe of the Concertgebouw (Concert Hall) whilst enjoying an international top concert or an exhilarating dance performance. Romantic souls throng the elegant City Theatre for an unforgettable night. Jazz enthusiasts feel at home at Art Centre De KAAP | De Werf, whereas the MaZ is the place to be for young people.

BRUGES CLASSICAL MUSIC CITY SOUNDS GREAT!

Bruges impresses first and foremost with its 'classics' in stone and its romantic cityscapes, but did you know that the city also has a particularly strong reputation in the field of classical music? This fame dates back to the Middle Ages, when the world-renowned Flemish polyphonists made a name for themselves in the city palaces of rich Burgundians. Nowadays, you can still experience the city to the rhythm of classical music.

For example, each week the Bruges carillon in the Belfry sends out sounds that can be heard across the entire city, while in Saint Saviour's Cathedral you can enjoy the softer tones of the centuries-old organ during the annual summer series of concerts. Music lovers can listen to musical masterpieces under the best possible conditions in the impressive Concert Hall, a building famed not only for its remarkable contemporary architecture, but also for its excellent acoustics. No-one knows this better than Anima Eterna Brugge, the Concert Hall's renowned symphonic house orchestra, which excels in performances played on period instruments. The city is also host to the celebrated MAfestival. Each summer, this famous early music festival presents a wide variety of concerts and activities in the historic setting of Bruges and its surrounding woodlands and wetlands.

What's more, the Concert Hall Circuit quite literally transforms Bruges into a tangible classical music city. By following an original experience path, you will learn how the concert hall really works *(Read more on page 60)*.

What's on the programme in 2019?

The following list summarizes the most important events in Bruges. Do you want to find out what's going on in Bruges during your stay in the city? Visit www.visitbruges.be and print off your own selection or drop by at one of the i tourist offices Markt (Historium), Stationsplein (station) and 't Zand (Concert Hall). The last office also sells tickets for events (and lots of other activities).

January

Bach Academie Brugge

16/1/2019 – 20/1/2019

In this ninth Bach Academy Brugge everything revolves around the relationship between heaven and earth, between the souls of the faithful and their redeeming Saviour. With new talents to discover and old stars to admire. And, of course, with the Collegium Vocale Ghent and Philippe Herreweghe.

INFO > www.concertgebouw.be

(You can read more about Bach and Early Music in the interview with Ayako Ito on page 115.)

Wintervonken (Winter Sparks)

25/1/2019 and 26/1/2019

Winter Sparks brings warmth and conviviality to the Burg square. The sixth edition of this winter festival once again guarantees scintillating street theatre, atmospheric concerts and heart-warming fire installations.

INFO > www.wintervonken.be

UNRAVEL THE SECRETS OF ANCIENT EGYPT

2/1/2019 – 5/1/2020

In the Bruges XpoCenter you can come face to face with real mummies and authentic artefacts during the exhibition *Mummies in Bruges – Secrets of Ancient Egypt*. The exhibition highlights the Egyptian concepts of life, death and the hereafter from the time of the pharaohs.

INFO > www.xpo-center-bruges.be

MURILLO, DE MENA AND ZURBARÁN MASTERS OF THE SPANISH BAROQUE

8/3/2019 – 6/10/2019

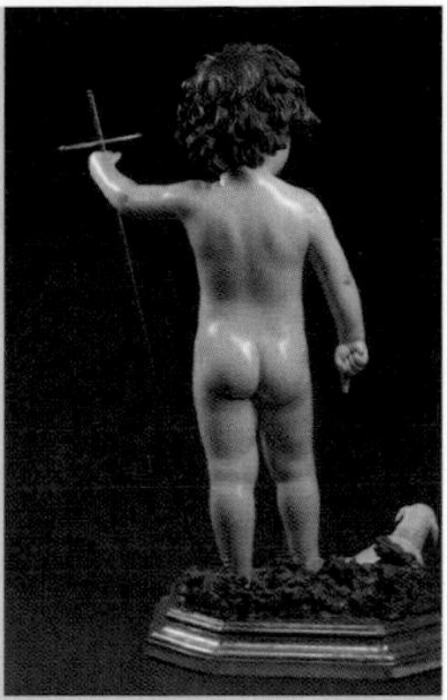

Saint John's Hospital will provide the backdrop for a selection of remarkable Spanish art from the 17th century. In the monumental hospital wards, some 20 works of sculpture and painting, full of Spanish passion, will be on display. It is a rare opportunity to become acquainted with some less well-known aspects of Spain's Golden Century. The highlight of the exhibition, in addition to paintings by famous Spanish masters like Murillo and Zurbarán, is a group of hyper-realistic sculptures by the greatest sculptor of the Spanish Baroque, Pedro De Mena. These outstanding exhibits, all belonging to private collections in Europe, will be on show in Bruges thanks to an international collaboration project with the Luxemburg National Museum for the History of Art.

INFO > www.museabrugge.be

February

Brugs Bierfestival (Bruges Beer Festival)

2/2/2019 and 3/2/2019

For a whole weekend long, Bruges is the places-to-beer, with a selection of some 400 top beers from 80 Belgian brewers. A delicious delight for your taste-buds!

INFO > www.brugsbierfestival.be

SLOW(36h)

23/2/2019 and 24/2/2019

SLOW(36h) gives you a full 36 hours to stop, stand still and relax, with (amongst other things) a performance of Bach's cello suites, a slow-walk through Bruges, an expressive route through the Concert Hall and mystical sufi music. Sample the joys of inertia and minimalism at their best.

INFO > www.concertgebouw.be

March

Bits of Dance

21/3/2019 – 23/3/2019

A dance festival where young dancers, choreographers and performers from home and abroad can show what they are made of. Because young talent deserves a stage. A must for every cultural explorer.

INFO > www.ccbrugge.be

Kosmos Festival

26/3/2019 – 10/4/2019

Marvel at the splendour of the universe and discover the remarkable similari-

A CENTURIES-OLD PROCESSION

30/5/2019

Each year on Ascension Day, the Holy Blood Procession takes place in Bruges in front of huge crowds. To begin with, members of the clergy, the brotherhoods and various costumed groups play out scenes from the Bible. This is followed by the story of the relic of the Holy Blood. In 1146, during the Second Crusade, Count Thierry of Alsace was able to obtain a few drops of the blood of Christ from the Patriarch of Jerusalem. This precious relic was brought to Bruges in 1150, where it has been venerated ever since in the Basilica of the Holy Blood.

ties between music and cosmology. For instance, NASA images are displayed to the accompaniment of magnificent orchestral music and live sounds from the universe guide six percussionists and four dancers through space.

INFO > www.concertgebouw.be

(You can read more about the dance performance 'The four elements', part of the Kosmos Festival, in the top five not-to-be-missed events of Ayako Ito on page 115.)

April

More Music!

10/4/2019 – 13/4/2019

The Bruges Concert Hall and the Cactus Music Centre once again join forces to make More Music!, an exciting encounter between diverse and contrasting musical worlds. The result is an intriguing total concept that takes the visitor on an adventurous voyage of musical discovery.

INFO > www.moremusicfestival.be

MOOOV-filmfestival

24/4/2019 – 2/5/2019

MOOOV once again offers the very best films from around the world in Cinema Lumière. From Argentine thrillers to South Korean humour: discover it all-in the heart of Bruges city centre!

INFO > www.mooov.be

May

Belmundo

15/5/2019 – 19/5/2019

Join this hip cultural trip to Spain, Portugal and Italy, with lots of music and extra activities.

INFO > www.ccbrugge.be

Budapest Festival

16/5/2019 – 18/5/2019

A music festival with concerts by the celebrated Budapest Festival Orchestra, conducted by Iván Fischer with romantic symphonies by Schubert and Bruckner and a piano work by Mozart.

INFO > www.concertgebouw.be *(You can read more about this festival on page 115, in the top five not-to-be-missed events of Ayako Ito.)*

Meifoor (May Fair)

10/5/2019 – 2/6/2019

For three fun-filled weeks some 90 fairground attractions 'take over' 't Zand and the Simon Stevinplein.

July

Cactusfestival

5/7/2019 – 7/7/2019

An atmospheric open-air music festival in the Minnewater Park, with a cocktail of contemporary music in all its diversity. Internationally famous, yet easy-going. A true people's festival that stimulates all senses, both onstage and off, with a large selection of culinary treats.

INFO > www.cactusfestival.be

Zandfeesten (Zand Festival)

7/7/2019

Flanders' largest antiques and second-hand market on 't Zand attracts bargain-hunters from far and wide.

Cirque Plus

12/7/2019 – 14/7/2019

A free circus festival featuring artists from home and abroad in a unique location: the garden of the Major Seminary.

INFO > www.cirqueplus.be

MOODS!

26/7/2019 – 3/8/2019

Musical and other fireworks at unforgettable locations in Bruges city centre, such as the Belfry courtyard and the Burg. In unique settings, you will be able to enjoy top national and international acts at one of the evening concerts.

INFO > www.moodsbrugge.be

August

MAfestival

2/8/2019 – 11/8/2019

Each year this highly respected festival of early music – MA stands for Musica Antiqua – continues to attract the world's top performers to Bruges and Bruges' wood- and wetlands.

INFO > www.mafestival.be

Zandfeesten (Zand Festival)

4/8/2019

Flanders' largest antiques and second-hand market on 't Zand.

Benenwerk (Leg-work) – Ballroom Brugeoise

10/8/2019

Put your best leg forward for a festival that is guaranteed to bring out the dancer in you. Spread across various locations in Bruges city centre, you will be swept along by live bands and DJs for a dance marathon at different ball-rooms, offering the most divergent dance music.

INFO > www.benenwerk.be

MAGNIFICENT CATHEDRAL CONCERTS

April to September

For more than 60 years, many renowned organists, choirs and soloists from both home and abroad have given the best of themselves during the cathedral concerts in St. Saviour's Cathedral *(also see page 72)*. Amongst others, Marcel Dupré, one of the greatest organ virtuosos of the 20th century, once played on the cathedral's centuries-old organ. Cultural pleasure of the highest quality. Not to be missed.

INFO > www.kathedraalconcerten.be

Brugse Kantdagen (Bruges Lace Days)

15/8/2019 – 18/8/2019

The Walplein and the buildings of the Halve Maan Brewery buzz with lace activities: information and exposition stands, lace sales and demonstrations.

INFO > www.kantcentrum.eu

(You read more about lace and the Lace Centre on page 66.)

Lichtfeest (Festival of Light)

16/8/2019 and 17/8/2019

Lissewege, the 'white polder village', once again wraps itself in a shroud of light and conviviality. As soon as evening falls, you can enjoy atmospheric music, video art, street theatre, fire and light installations, etc.

INFO > www.lichtfeestlissewege.be

September

Open Monumentendag (Open Monument Day)

7/9/2019 and 8/9/2019

During the second weekend of September, Bruges organises the 31th edition of Open Monument Day, when it opens the doors of its many monuments to the general public.

INFO > www.bruggeomd.be

Zandfeesten (Zand Festival)

22/9/2019

Antiques and second-hand market on 't Zand.

Kookeet (Cook-Eat)

28/9/2019 – 30/9/2019

The 9th edition of Kookeet is organized in a stylish tented village. During this culinary event, 31 top chefs from in and around Bruges and one guest chef serve gastronomic dishes at reasonable prices *(also see page 91)*.

INFO > www.kookeet.be

CARILLON CONCERTS

Throughout the year, you can enjoy free, live carillon concerts in Bruges on Wednesdays, Saturdays and Sundays from 11.00 a.m. to 12.00 p.m. From mid-June to mid-September, evening concerts also take place on Mondays and Wednesdays from 9.00 p.m. to 10.00 p.m. The inner courtyard of the Belfry is a good place to listen.

INFO > www.carillon-brugge.be

October

Iedereen klassiek (Everyone Classic)

26/10/2019

Classical music radio station Klara and the Concert Hall join forces to allow you to explore the beauty of Bach, Beethoven and Bruges. This festival is traditionally brought to a close with a performance by the Brussels Philharmonic Orchestra.

INFO > www.concertgebouw.be

November

Wintermarkt (Winter market)

22/11/2019 – 1/1/2020

For more than a month, you can immerse yourself in the true Christmas atmosphere on the Market Square and at the Simon Stevinplein; on the Market Square you can even pull on your ice skates.

December

December Dance

6/12/2019 – 16/12/2019

The annual rendezvous for dance lovers from all over the world. Over a number of days, this festival brings together established names and young talent at a range of unique locations in the city. The Brussels performing arts collective Needcompany and Jan Lauwers are the central guest and curator of the 2019 edition.

INFO > www.decemberdance.be

All dates and events are subject to possible change.

Cultural temples

17 Concertgebouw (Concert Hall)

This international music and art centre is a place that offers the very best in contemporary dance and classical music. The impressive Concert Auditorium (1,289 seats) and intimate Chamber Music Hall (322 seats) are famed for their excellent acoustics. In the Concert Hall, you can also admire various contemporary works of art. And why not take a look behind the scenes during the day by following the Concertgebouw Circuit *(see pages 60 and 114)*.

INFO AND TICKETS > 't Zand 34, opening hours of the Concertgebouw Circuit or tel. +32 (0)70 22 12 12 (Monday to Friday, 2.00 p.m.-5.00 p.m.), www.concertgebouw.be

28 KAAP | De Werf

KAAP Creative Compass, the centre for contemporary art, supports creative talent in Bruges at two separate locations: De Werf and De Groenplaats. In De Groenplaats, young artists and performers can develop their work in peaceful and quiet surroundings. De Werf is the place for anyone who loves exciting theatre and swinging jazz from the four corners of the world. But KAAP also likes to go out onto the streets, filling the city's open spaces with public and performers. KAAP is your creative compass for Bruges.

INFO AND TICKETS > Werfstraat 108, tel. +32 (0)70 22 12 12 (Monday to Friday, 2.00 p.m.-5.00 p.m.), www.kaap.be

Concert Hall

City Theatre

31 Magdalenazaal (MaZ, Magdalena Concert Hall)

Its 'black-box' architecture means that the MaZ is the ideal location for all kinds of events. The Bruges Cultural Centre and the Cactus Music Festival both organize pop and rock concerts here, with major artists from the world of music and more intimate club talents. Rising stars in the theatrical and dance arts also perform in this perfect setting. Children's and family events are regular features on the programme.
INFO AND TICKETS > Magdalenastraat 27, Sint-Andries, tel. +32 (0)50 44 30 60 (Tuesday to Friday, 1.00 p.m.-5.00 p.m. and Saturday, 4.00 p.m.-7.00 p.m., closed 1/7 to 15/8 and on public holidays), www.ccbrugge.be

41 Stadsschouwburg (City Theatre)

The Bruges City Theatre (1869), one of Europe's best preserved city theatres, celebrates its 150th birthday this year. The sober yet majestic neo-Renaissance facade of this royal theatre conceals a palatial foyer and an equally magnificent red and gold auditorium. This outstanding infrastructure is used for performances of contemporary dance and theatre and for concerts of various kinds.
INFO AND TICKETS > Vlamingstraat 29, tel. +32 (0)50 44 30 60 (Tuesday to Friday, 1.00 p.m.-5.00 p.m. and Saturday 4.00 p.m.-7.00 p.m., closed 1/7 to 15/8 and on public holidays), www.ccbrugge.be

Shopping in Bruges

Hoogstraat

Although Bruges is often associated with the virtuosity and mastery of craftsmen from the past, today's city is still a breeding ground for creative entrepreneurs of all kinds. Here you can find dozens of authentic shops, each offering that little something extra, while often nestling alongside the more traditional and reputed art galleries and antique emporia. Shopping in Bruges is a veritable voyage of discovery, ranging from original and trendy newcomers, through vintage addresses that exude nostalgia, to classic establishments that have been run by the same family for generations.

IN THE SPOTLIGHT

HANDMADE IN BRUGES
A CITY OF INSPIRING CRAFTSMEN (AND WOMEN)

Bruges is full of passionate and highly motivated creative spirits, who day after day prove that craftsmanship has a future and that Bruges' craftsmanship is timeless. Modern-day artisans who produce their wares locally and by hand are recognized with the award of the Handmade in Bruges label. The Handmade in Bruges guide (available in Dutch, French, German and English and available for free from the i tourist offices) bundles together these 'makers of things', putting them both literally and figuratively on the map, allowing you to find your way with ease to one of their many Handmade stores or workshops. And once you are there, you are almost certain to leave with an original, handmade gift – either for yourself or for your family and friends at home.

Make sure you also visit De Makersrepubliek at Academiestraat 14, an open house for Bruges craftsmen, young entrepreneurs and start-ups. The home to Handmade in Bruges is situated Sint-Jakobsstraat 36 (www.handmadeinbrugge.be). *For more inspiring shops and stores, take a look at pages 121 and 130, where you can find everything you need to know about #LocalLove and #ArtandAntiques.*

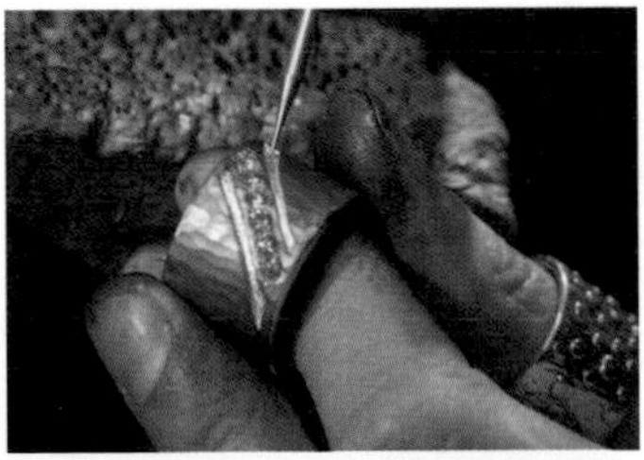

Where to shop?

Because Bruges is pedestrian-friendly and the main streets are all close to each other, a day's shopping here is a relaxing experience. You will find all the major national and international chains, as well as trendy local boutiques and plenty of interesting new discoveries. The most important shopping streets (indicated in yellow on the removable city map) run between the Market Square and the old city gates. There is also a small but elegant shopping centre, the Zilverpand, between Noordzandstraat and Zuidzandstraat. In Steenstraat, you will find the famous brand names, whereas Langestraat boasts many little second-hand and bric-à-brac shops. The large hypermarkets are located just outside the city centre.

When to shop?

Most shops operate from Monday to Saturday, opening at 10.00 a.m. and closing at either 6.00 or 6.30 p.m. But even on Sundays you don't need to leave Bruges empty-handed. Many specialist stores are open on Sundays as well. And on 'Shopping Sundays' – the first Sunday of the month, from 1.00 p.m. to 6.00 p.m., except on public holidays – they are joined by many of the other shops. There is restricted access for traffic on Saturday afternoon and 'Shopping Sundays' (from 1.00 p.m. to 6.00 p.m.) in the following shopping streets: Zuidzandstraat, Steenstraat, Geldmuntstraat and Noordzandstraat.

TIP

Looking for fun shopping addresses? You can find them in the chapter 'Tips from Bruges experts', pages 102-103, 110-111, 118-119, 126-127 and 134-135.

Typical Bruges souvenirs

Bruges was a flourishing centre of the diamond trade as early as the 14th century, and the city also boasted several professional diamond-cutting establishments. In the diamond laboratory of the Bruges Diamond Museum, you will learn how all that sparkling splendour is assessed and processed. After that, it's only a matter of checking out the museum shop or the many other jewellery stores in the city with a keen connoisseur's eye before making your move – and cashing in. *You can find more information about the Bruges Diamond Museum on page 61.*

Since time immemorial, lace has also been inextricably connected to Bruges. Once upon a time, as many as a quarter

of all the women in the city were employed making lace. Nowadays, you can still see female lace-makers in action in several of the Bruges lace shops. *You can find more information about lace and the Lace Centre on page 66.*

The people of Bruges have always liked a glass or two of good beer. The city boasts several excellent locally made ales – *Straffe Hendrik* and *Brugse Zot*, both brewed by De Halve Maan Brewery, right in the heart of the historic city centre – as well as eight traditional-style beers, including the *Fort Lapin 8 Triple* and the *Fort Lapin 10 Quadruple*, both brewed in the Fort Lapin Brewery on the edge of the city, and the *Bourgogne des Flanders*, which you can sample in the brewery of the same name along the Dijver. Have we convinced you? Then why not visit the annual Bruges Beer Festival or the Bruges Beer Experience on the Markt. *You can find more information about the Halve Maan and Bourgogne des Flandres breweries and the Bruges Beer Experience on pages 57-59; more information about the Fort Lapin brewery on www.fortlapin.com; more information about the Bruges Beer Festival on page 79.*

Perhaps you are not such a fan of beer? Those with a sweet tooth can visit one of more than 50 chocolate boutiques that cater to all tastes: from deliciously old-fashioned chocolate blocks, through finger-licking good pralines that melt in your mouth, to ingenious molecular chocolate preparations tailored to the requirements of the city's star chefs. Did you know that Bruges can boast both its own city praline (the Brugsch Swaentje – Bruges Swan – which local people voted to be the tastiest from a selection of candidates) and its own city chocolate (Sjokla, based on fair trade cocoa)? *Read more about chocolate on page 59-60.*

Sjokla

Gastronomic Bruges

With its impressive number of top-quality restaurants, Bruges is a paradise for gastronomes. The range of culinary excellence on offer varies from Michelin-star cooking to stylish local brasseries serving good and honest (inter)national specialities.

KOOKEET
A MAJOR CULINARY FESTIVAL, WITH TOP BRUGES CHEFS AND A GUEST CHEF

Each year, more than 100,000 people visit the Kookeet culinary festival, which this year celebrates its ninth edition. The recipe for success? For three days, top Bruges chefs and one guest chef serve up gastronomic gems at reasonable prices. The visitors can put together their own menus at their own pace. The participating Bruges chefs are all top names in their field and have one or more Michelin stars, a mention in Bib Gourmand or a high score in Gault&Millau.

You can find more info on page 82 and on www.kookeet.be.

Award winning restaurants

- » **De Jonkman** Maalse Steenweg 438, 8310 Sint-Kruis, tel. +32 (0)50 36 07 67, www.dejonkman.be (2 Michelin-stars, 18/20 graded by Gault&Millau)
- » **Zet'Joe** Langestraat 11, 8000 Brugge, tel. +32 (0)50 33 82 59, www.zetjoe.be (1 Michelin-star, 17/20 graded by Gault&Millau)
- » **Sans Cravate** Langestraat 159, 8000 Brugge, tel. +32 (0)50 67 83 10, www.sanscravate.be (1 Michelin-star, 16.5/20 graded by Gault&Millau)
- » **Den Gouden Harynck** Groeninge 25, 8000 Brugge, tel. +32 (0)50 33 76 37, www.goudenharynck.be (1 Michelin-star, 16/20 graded by Gault&Millau)
- » **Goffin** Maalse Steenweg 2, 8310 Sint-Kruis, tel. +32 (0)50 68 77 88, www.timothygoffin.be (1 Michelinster, 15.5/20 graded by Gault&Millau)
- » **Auberge De Herborist** De Watermolen 15, 8200 Sint-Andries, tel. +32 (0)50 38 76 00, www.aubergedeherborist.be (1 Michelinster, 15/20 graded by Gault&Millau)
- » **Bistro Bruut** Meestraat 9, 8000 Brugge, tel. +32 (0)50 69 55 09, www.bistrobruut.be (15.5/20 graded by Gault&Millau)
- » **L.E.S.S.** Torhoutse Steenweg 479, 8200 Sint-Michiels, tel. +32 (0)50 69 93 69, www.l-e-s-s.be (15/20 graded by Gault&Millau)
- » **Patrick Devos** Zilverstraat 41, 8000 Brugge, tel. +32 (0)50 33 55 66, www.patrickdevos.be (15/20 graded by Gault&Millau)
- » **Rock-Fort** Langestraat 15-17, 8000 Brugge, tel. +32 (0)50 33 41 13, www.rock-fort.be (15/20 graded by Gault&Millau)
- » **Floris** Gistelse Steenweg 520, 8200 Sint-Andries, tel. +32 (0)50 73 60 20, www.florisrestaurant.be (14.5/20 graded by Gault&Millau)
- » **Tête Pressée** Koningin Astridlaan 100, 8200 Sint-Michiels, tel. +32 (0)470 21 26 27, www.tetepressee.be (14.5/20 graded by Gault&Millau)
- » **Bistro Refter** Molenmeers 2, 8000 Brugge, tel. +32 (0)50 44 49 00, www.bistrorefter.be (14/20 graded by Gault&Millau and selected as a Bib Gourmand)
- » **bonte B** Dweersstraat 12, 8000 Brugge, tel. +32 (0)50 34 83 43, www.restaurantbonteb.be (14/20 graded by Gault&Millau)
- » **Franco Belge** Langestraat 109, 8000 Brugge, tel. +32 (0)50 69 56 48, www.restaurantfrancobelge.be (14/20 graded by Gault&Millau)
- » **Hubert Gastrobar** Langestraat 155, 8000 Brugge, tel. +32 (0)50 64 10 09, www.gastrobar-hubert.be (14/20 graded by Gault&Millau)
- » **Le Mystique** Niklaas Desparsstraat 11, 8000 Brugge, tel. +32 (0)50 44 44 45, www.lemystique.be (14/20 graded by Gault&Millau)
- » **'t Pandreitje** Pandreitje 6, 8000 Brugge, tel. +32 (0)50 33 11 90, www.pandreitje.be (14/20 graded by Gault&Millau)
- » **Tanuki** Oude Gentweg 1, 8000 Brugge, tel. +32 (0)50 34 75 12, www.tanuki.be (14/20 graded by Gault&Millau)

- » **Assiette Blanche** Philipstockstraat 23-25, 8000 Brugge, tel. +32 (0)50 34 00 94, www.assietteblanche.be (13.5/20 graded by Gault&Millau and selected as a Bib Gourmand)
- » **Bistro Rombaux** Moerkerkse Steenweg 139, 8310 Sint-Kruis, tel. +32 (0)50 73 79 49, www.bistrorombaux.be (13/20 graded by Gault&Millau)
- » **Cantine Copine** Steenkaai 34, 8000 Brugge, tel. +32 (0)470 97 04 55, www.cantinecopine.be (13/20 graded by Gault&Millau)
- » **De Mangerie** Oude Burg 20, 8000 Brugge, tel. +32 (0)50 33 93 36, www.mangerie.com (13/20 graded by Gault&Millau)
- » **Goesepitte 43** Goezeputstraat 43, 8000 Brugge, tel. +32 (0)50 66 02 23, www.goesepitte43.be (13/20 graded by Gault&Millau)
- » **Kok au Vin** Ezelstraat 21, 8000 Brugge, tel. +32 (0)50 33 95 21, www.kok-au-vin.be (13/20 graded by Gault&Millau and selected as a Bib Gourmand)
- » **Komtuveu** Gentpoortstraat 51, 8000 Brugge, tel. +32 (0)495 62 53 29, www.komtuveu.com (13/20 graded by Gault&Millau)
- » **La Buena Vista** Sint-Clarastraat 43, 8000 Brugge, tel. +32 (0)50 33 38 96 (13/20 graded by Gault&Millau)
- » **La Tâche** Blankenbergse Steenweg 1, 8000 Sint-Pieters, tel. +32 (0)50 68 02 52, www.latache.be (13/20 graded by Gault&Millau)
- » **Lieven** Philipstockstraat 45, 8000 Brugge, tel. +32 (0)50 68 09 75, www.etenbijlieven.be (13/20 graded by Gault&Millau)
- » **'t Jong Gerecht** Langestraat 119, 8000 Brugge, tel. +32 (0)50 31 32 32, www.tjonggerecht.be (13/20 graded by Gault&Millau)
- » **Parkrestaurant** Minderbroedersstraat 1, 8000 Brugge, tel. +32 (0)497 80 18 72, www.parkrestaurant.be (12/20 graded by Gault&Millau)
- » **The Blue Lobster** Tijdokstraat 9, 8380 Zeebrugge, tel. +32 (0)50 68 45 71, www.thebluelobster.be (12/20 graded by Gault&Millau)
- » **Tom's Diner** West-Gistelhof 23, 8000 Brugge, tel. +32 (0)50 33 33 82, www.tomsdiner.be (12/20 graded by Gault&Millau)
- » **Tou.Gou** Smedenstraat 47, 8000 Brugge, tel. +32 (0)50 70 58 02, www.tougou.be (12/20 graded by Gault&Millau and selected as a Bib Gourmand)
- » **'t Werftje** Werfkaai 29, 8380 Zeebrugge, tel. +32 (0)497 55 30 10, www.twerftje.be (12/20 graded by Gault&Millau)

More tips on finding the right address for you can be found in the section 'Tips from Bruges experts', pages 100-101, 108-109, 116-117, 124-125, 132-133.

Markt

Tips from **Bruges experts**

Bruges, world heritage city

Sonia Papili reveals the Italian side of Bruges

Rozenhoedkaai

During the week, Italian Sonia Papili studies the North Sea with academic sobriety; during the weekend, she guides her fellow countrymen with great passion around her adopted city. A passion that began gradually some thirteen years ago, but now burns more brightly than ever.

ID-CARD

Name: Sonia Papili
Nationality: Italian
Date of birth: 17 May 1972
Has lived in Bruges since 2006. Sonia is a geologist with the Ministry of Defence and a tourist guide in Bruges.

Two geologists – him attached to the University of Ghent, her attached to the University of Rome – who met on a ship in Istanbul to discuss climate change: there are worse ways to start a long-distance relationship. For three years, the pair commuted back and forth between Italy and Belgium before finally deciding to settle in Bruges.
'I had only been in Bruges once before,' says Sonia. 'I was much more familiar with Ghent, but my husband thought that Bruges better suited my personality and temperament. And he was right: Bruges really is my city!' In the meantime, Sonia learnt Dutch and started work here as a geologist. During her citizenship programme, she became more and more curious about the history of her new home town. 'During the language course they told us a little bit about the history of the place. This intrigued me and so I decided to take a three-year course to become an official guide in Bruges.'

'I was much more familiar with Ghent, but my husband thought that Bruges better suited my personality and temperament. And he was right: Bruges really is my city!'

WHY BRUGES IS A WORLD HERITAGE CITY

In 1998, the Bruges Beguinage was recognized as a world heritage site. A year later, the Belfry received similar recognition. In 2000, this was extended to cover the entire city centre. Since 2009, the Holy Blood Procession has been listed as an item of immaterial world heritage. Bruges also has a valuable and impressive architectural patrimony and is a fine example of an architecturally harmonious city. In particular, Bruges is famed for its Gothic style buildings in brick. In addition, its authentic and organically developed medieval urban fabric has been perfectly preserved and it is also the 'birthplace' of the Flemish primitives. In other words, reasons enough for UNESCO to label Bruges as a 'world heritage city'.

XPLORE BRUGES – The official city tour app of Bruges

You can discover all the secrets of Bruges with the free Xplore Bruges-app. There are city walks, cycling circuits and visits to indoor attractions. Almost all the routes are available in five languages: English, Dutch, French, German and Spanish. At the moment, there are sixteen different routes: from 'Bruges, anno 1562', through 'The hidden treasures of St. James's Church', to 'Handmade in Bruges'. In short, something for everyone!

Tip: download the app at home or from any wifi network, you no longer need access to mobile internet. If you are not familiar with downloading apps, check out the routes on the website www.xplorebruges.be.

Italian art

During her guide training, Sonia soon discovered that she was not the first Italian to lose her heart to Bruges. From the 13th to the 15th century, Bruges was an international trading centre that had close links with Europe's other great trading cities. This also meant with the great Italian cities, which around 1300 had decided to focus on international trade by sea as the best way to achieve fame and fortune, and saw Bruges as an ideal base for their activities in Northern Europe. Inspired by the success of the Italian merchants, the traders of other countries soon found their way to Bruges, which grew steadily to become the full-fledged, commercial counterpart of Venice. The 'Venice of the North' was born, although you could just as easily argue that Venice is the 'Bruges of the South'. 'A fine discovery for me, and one which made me look at the city – and in particular its Italian quarter – in a new light.'

'It is now widely known that the Italians traded here,' says Sonia, 'but they also left behind traces of their artistic herit-

age.' Sonia's thesis for her guide's training course dealt with the works of Italian art that can still be found in Bruges. 'Of course, there is the *Madonna and Child* by Michelangelo in the Church of Our Lady, but there are many other Italian masterpieces to admire as well. I am thinking of the poetic *Veins of the Convent* by Giuseppe Penone in the Old St. John site. Or the three works by the contemporary artist Mario Molinari, who is famous in Italy, one of which is in the Kustlaan in Zeebrugge, near the old fish auction site. I also suspect that the beautiful medallions of Lorenzo de' Medici and his wife Clarice Orsini in the Bladelin Court were made in Italy, but I have found no evidence for this so far.'
'What is beyond doubt is the fact that de' Medici, a family of 15th century Florentine bankers, did once run a bank from the Bladelin Court. I am also very impressed by the most recent statues on the facade of the City Hall. These were carved in the 1980s by Stefaan Depuydt (1937-2016) and his Italian wife, Livia Canestraro. Two of the statues are self-portraits of the couple. In fact, there are lots of places in Bruges where you can discover their work. They are a testimony to how beautiful and successful artistic collaboration between differing nationalities can sometimes be.'

Starting young

Nowadays, Sonia passes on her love for Bruges to her former compatriots. 'Of course, the Italians love it when they are guided around the city in their own language. It is very often their first visit to Bruges, and because I understand them perhaps a little bit better than other guides, I can also show them a little bit more of the things that really interest them. Naturally, they first want to know what it's like to live here, about the schools and the medical system, about people's attitudes to work and leisure... With my hand on my heart, I can assure them that life here is really good.'

Veins of the Convent

In the meantime, Sonia's own family also know where to find all the best places in Bruges. 'The city continues to evolve. As soon as anything new appears, I immediately want to check it out. In this way, my three daughters also get to share in my love of Bruges from an early age!'
(If you want to discover the beauty of Bruges with an official guide, please turn to pages 48-49.)

Sonia Papili's
best addresses

FAVOURITE SPOT

» **Coupure**

'I am a big fan of the **Coupure**, a spot in the middle of the city but a million miles away from all the hustle and bustle. The way in which the majestic rows of trees draw a green line along Coupure canal is pure art. What's more, our family is linked to the Coupure in a very special way.'

RESTAURANTS

» **La Tâche**, Blankenbergse Steenweg 1, tel. +32 (0)50 68 02 52, www.latache.be

'My husband went to eat here a few times and was always full of praise for the food. The restaurant – housed in a beautiful city mansion – is known for its classic cooking laced with the flavours of the South. That's why La Tâche is at the top of my 'must visit' list.'

» **Sans Cravate**, Langestraat 159, tel. +32 (0)50 67 83 10, www.sanscravate.be

'Our absolute favourite. Sans Cravate now has a star – and fully deserved. It's not somewhere we go every month, but if we have something special to celebrate, then we like to do it here! Chef Henk prepares both classic and contemporary dishes.'

» **De Schaar**, Hooistraat 2, tel. +32 (0)50 33 59 79, www.bistrodeschaar.be
'This is the perfect place for anyone who wants to enjoy to the full the Coupure – my favourite place in the city. In the summer, it's wonderful to just sit on a terrace at the water's edge; in the winter, you can enjoy the lovely open fire inside.'

» **De Bottelier**, Sint-Jakobsstraat 63, tel. +32 (0)50 33 18 60, www.debottelier.com
'This is a real no-nonsense address with healthy cooking focused mainly on vegetables. And reasonably priced as well! Add to this a charming interior and you will soon understand why the sign 'full' often hangs in the window.'

» **Du Phare**, Sasplein 2, tel. +32 (0)50 34 35 90, www.duphare.be
'After a pleasant summer walk along the ramparts or a climb up one of the windmill hills, there is nothing nicer than getting your breath back on the large sun terrace of Du Phare. And if the weather is not kind, you can enjoy the elegant interior of this top-class bistro with its seasonal, international cuisine.'

CAFÉS

» **Café Rose Red**, Cordoeaniersstraat 16, tel. +32 (0)50 33 90 51, www.caferosered.com
'To be honest, I am not a big drinker, more a sipper and a taster. And there is no better place to do this than in Café Rose Red, with its fine range of the very best Belgian beers. They have dozens of them!'

» **De Belleman Pub**, Jozef Suvéestraat 22, tel. +32 (0)50 34 19 89
'Local people affectionately call this traditional brown café on the corner of the Koningin Astridpark 'The Belleman's'. I love the classic British pub-atmosphere and the fact that you can chat to locals who have sat at the same place at the bar for years and years.'

» **De Proeverie**, Katelijnestraat 6, tel. +32 (0)50 33 08 87, www.deproeverie.be
'The best hot chocolate in Bruges comes from this British-style tearoom. Freshly melted chocolate with warm milk: what more can you want? Perhaps something from their delicious selection of homemade ice-creams, cupcakes and scones! A visit to De Proeverie is always lip-licking good!'

» **De Zolder**, Vlamingstraat 53, tel. +32 (0)477 24 49 05
'A cellar cafe named 'De Zolder', which means 'attic' in Dutch: it could only happen in Belgium! De Zolder is a cool and relaxing café, where you can sample local beers in wonderful medieval surroundings. Ideal for a night-out with a group of friends.'

» **Grand Hotel Casselbergh**, Hoogstraat 6, tel. +32 (0)50 44 65 00, www.grandhotelcasselbergh.com
'The elegant bar of the Grand Hotel Casselbergh is a great place to chill out before or after your evening dinner. You can sit at the bar counter or lounge in one of the deliciously comfortable easy chairs. This is the place to start or round off your evening on the town in style. People not staying at the hotel are always more than welcome.'

SHOPPING LIST

» **Callebert**, Wollestraat 25, tel. +32 (0)50 33 50 61, www.callebert.be
'As a design freak, I can always find something to set my pulse racing at Callebert, a style oasis where timeless beauty reigns supreme. Complete with a children's department that will tempt the adults as well!'

» **Da Vinci**, Geldmuntstraat 34, tel. +32 (0)50 33 36 50, www.davinci-brugge.be
'It doesn't matter if the weather is freezing cold or boiling hot: there are always visitors lined up in droves outside this deluxe ice-cream parlour. The number of different flavours is almost beyond belief. What's more, everything – from the ice-cream right down to the sauces – is made on the premises.'

» **De Witte Pelikaan**, Vlamingstraat 23, tel. +32 (0)50 34 82 84, www.dewittepelikaan.be

'Whoever loves Christmas will love De Witte Pelikaan, with its year-round selection of Christmas baubles and jingle bells. Christmas trees everywhere, full of craft-made glassware, special Christmas baubles and ornaments ranging from cheap and cheerful to super-deluxe. If you don't find the Christmas decorations of your dreams here, you won't find them anywhere!'

» **Krokodil**, Sint-Jakobsstraat 47, tel. +32 (0)50 33 75 79, www.krokodil.be
'A regular port-of-call for people with kids. This is not the place for 'throwaway' junk, but for beautiful and solidly made toys that will stand the test of time.'

» **BbyB**, Sint-Amandsstraat 39, tel. +32 (0)50 70 57 60, www.bbyb.be
'At BbyB you can find a range of elegantly sleek haute couture chocolates that are almost impossible to resist. Time after time I am tempted by this classy concept store to try out new and exciting flavour combinations. Because let's admit it: who can say 'no' to chocolate with rhubarb, speculoos biscuit, 'babulettes' or star anise?'

SECRET TIP

» **The remains of the old St. Donatian Cathedral**, Burg 10, tel. +32 (0)50 44 68 44

'Under the prestigious Crowne Plaza Hotel lay hidden the remains of the **St. Donatian Cathedral**, which during the Middle Ages represented the ecclesiastical power of the Church on the Burg square. St. Donatian's was the court church of the counts of Flanders. If you really want to dig into the oldest parts of the city's historic past, ask at the reception desk if you can take a look in their cellar. Because in Bruges, the ground is always full of history.'

Flemish primitives in the spotlight

Centuries-old masterpieces still thrill Till-Holger Borchert

Groeningemuseum

He was born in Hamburg and recently moved from Brussels to Bruges, where he has already worked for the past 18 years. Surrounded by six centuries of fine art, he still finds huge pleasure in the magnificence of the Flemish Primitives. In 2002, Till-Holger Borchert was one of the curators of Bruges, Cultural Capital of Europe. Today he is director-general of Musea Brugge and chief curator of the Groeninge Museum and the Arentshuis.

ID-CARD

Name: Till-Holger Borchert
Nationality: German
Date of birth: 4 January 1967
This director-general of Musea Brugge and chief curator of the Groeninge Museum lives and works in Bruges. He is the author of countless publications on the Flemish primitives.

'Bruges is an exceptionally beautiful city,' says Till-Holger Borchert. 'What's more, it is also a wonderfully liveable place, partly because of the clever and careful way in which the city has been able to mix her medieval character with a modern ambiance. As early as the 13th century, the concentration of wealthy citizens enabled Bruges to become the commercial heart of northwestern Europe. In the 15th century, the Burgundian authorities took successful structural measures, which resulted in an increase of the population and had a positive effect on the city's further development. Just as importantly, Bruges was spared the many ravages of the so-called Iconoclastic Fury, which caused so much damage in other cities. That spirit of respect and tolerance still pervades the city today. I must say it is a great joy to be here. The countless locals and visitors will surely fully agree with me.'

Madonnas from around the Corner

'Nearly every day I go and greet two masterpieces: Hans Memling's *Madonna and Maarten van Nieuwenhove* at the Saint John's Hospital and Jan van Eyck's *Madonna with Canon Joris van der Paele* at the Groeninge Museum. I am not saying that I discover something new every time I look at them, but my curiosity and my pleasure remain as great as ever. And I still try and find out

'Nearly every day I go and greet two masterpieces.'

new things about them. They just continue to fascinate me! I sometimes wonder why people from all corners of the world have always found the Flemish primitives so absorbing. The answer perhaps lies in the fact that for the very first time in art history we are confronted with recognisable people and familiar objects that correspond to today's reality. Even a Madonna seems to look like the woman from around the corner. The Flemish primitives laid the foundation of an artistic concept that in its realism is perfectly recognisable and therefore understandable to a modern-day observer. The Flemish primitives discovered the individual. Quite a feat. Those Flemish painters were also dab hands at solving problems. They explored space in an incredibly skilful and sophisticated way, for example by placing a mirror somewhere in the room. In Memling's diptych, a round mirror on the left-hand

side behind the Madonna reflects the interior she is sitting in. In it, her own portrait is painted just a whisker away from the silhouette of the patrician Maarten van Nieuwenhove, Memling's patron. Truly magnificent. Are these works of art still capable of moving me? Absolutely. For pure emotion, a painter like Rogier van der Weyden touches me more deeply than Jan van Eyck. The works of van Eyck or Memling impress

GRUUTHUSE AMAZES AS NEVER BEFORE

2019 is the year of the Gruuthuse Museum. This luxurious 15th century city palace reopens its doors at the end of May. Following a long period of renovation, the building is now fully prepared to once again amaze its visitors, just as it did centuries ago when the lords of Gruuthuse still lived there. The museum's exhibits tell the story of 500 years of fascinating Bruges history through a rich collection of art objects, documents and manuscripts, which bring the rulers of the past and the city's rich elite to life. The museum also gives access to the authentic prayer chapel, which connects the Gruuthuse Palace with the Church of Our Lady. From this unique chapel, the palace residents could take part in religious services in comfort and privacy, without having to mingle with the common people.
Discover more about the Gruuthuse Musuem on page 64.

me more with their intellectual and conceptual qualities. Van der Weyden and van Eyck: it is worth visiting the treasure houses of Bruges, even if only for the pleasure of enjoying these two opposite ends of the artistic spectrum.'

INTERESTING TOMBS

The central feature in the Jerusalem Chapel – located in the Saint-Anne district – is the ceremonial tomb of Anselm Adornes (1424-1483) and his wife, Margareta Vander Banck (d. 1462). Anselm – scion of a wealthy merchant family, confidant of the dukes of Burgundy and a counsellor of the King of Scotland – had this chapel built in the likeness of the Church of the Holy Sepulchre in Jerusalem, with the intention that he should be buried here with his spouse. However, Anselm was killed and buried in Scotland. Only his heart was later added to the tomb in Bruges.
Learn more about the Adornes on page 54.

Till-Holger Borchert's **best addresses**

FAVOURITE SPOT

» **The churches of Bruges**

'The great churches of Bruges possess wonderful art collections, containing pieces that wouldn't disgrace any top museum. Look up at the sheer breath-taking height of the Church of Our Lady, whose 115.5-metre high tower is the second tallest brick-built tower in the world. When in Saint Saviour's, do go and marvel at the frescoes in the baptistery. And Saint-James's Church is worth its while for the impressive **mausoleum of the de Gros family**, because this sculptural masterpiece reveals par excellence the self-confidence and power of the Burgundian elite.'

RESTAURANTS

» **Kok au Vin**, Ezelstraat 21, tel. +32 (0)50 33 95 21, www.kok-au-vin.be

'In this pleasant bistro you can enjoy great cooking with local and super-fresh products. Chef Jürgen Aerts is a master of combining flavors, simply but deliciously. What's more, eating here is very affordable.'

» **Den Gouden Harynck**, Groeninge 25, tel. +32 (0)50 33 76 37, www.goudenharynck.be

'Den Gouden Harynck is a household name in Bruges, known and loved by foodies of all kinds. It is also one of the most pleasant star-rated restaurants in the city – as anyone who has ever been there will tell you.'

» **Den Amand**, Sint-Amandsstraat 4, tel. +32 (0)50 34 01 22, www.denamand.be

'In Den Amand, I once saw a German restaurant critic copy out the entire menu. You can't get higher praise than that! A small and elegant bistro, where you will find both visitors and local people enjoying the excellent food.'

» **'t Schrijverke**, Gruuthusestraat 4, tel. +32 (0)50 33 29 08, www.tschrijverke.be

'This homely restaurant is named after a poem by Guido Gezelle, which hangs in a place of honour next to the door. But 't Schrijverke is above all rightly famed for its delicious regional dishes and its *Karmeliet* beer on tap.'

» **Tanuki**, Oude Gentweg 1, tel. +32 (0)50 34 75 12, www.tanuki.be

'A true temple of food where you immediately drop your voice to the level of a whisper, so that you don't disturb the silent enjoyment of the other diners. In the open kitchen the chef does magical things with sushi and sashimi, and prepares his seven course menus with true oriental serenity.'

CAFÉS

» **Café 't Klein Venetië**, Braambergstraat 1, tel. +32 (0)50 33 10 37, www.kleinvenetie.be

'Every Bruges local knows that if you want to enjoy the sun, the terrace of Café 't Klein Venetië is the best place to go. I like to sit here on the front row, enjoying the busy crowds on the Huidenvettersplein and the magnificent view over the Rozenhoedkaai, the most photographed spot in Bruges. In short, when you are on this super-popular terrace, you never know where to look first.'

» **Café Marcel**, Niklaas Desparsstraat 7-9, tel. +32 (0)50 33 55 02, www.hotelmarcel.be

'Café Marcel is Bruges' refined version of a contemporary vintage café, but in a tight, new design setting. Think of dark wooden floorboards, simple lamps, leather benches and original wood panelling. You can pop in here for a tasty breakfast or an aperitif with tapas.'

» **Delaney's Irish Pub & Restaurant**, Burg 8, tel. +32 (0)50 34 91 45, www.delaneys.be

'It's always party time in this Irish pub, with its distinctive international atmosphere. Delaney's is the kind of place where you can rub shoulders with the whole world at the bar.'

» **The Druid's Cellar**, Sint-Amandsstraat 11, tel. +32 (0)50 61 41 44, www.thedruidscellar.eu

'I like to drop in at The Druid's Cellar every now and again, even if only to watch Drew, my favourite barkeeper, in action. Or simply to relax and enjoy a glass from their wide range of Scottish and Irish whiskies. They always taste just that little bit better in The Druid's.'

» **Hollandse Vismijn**, Vismarkt 4, tel. +32 (0)50 33 33 01

'Whenever I fancy one of the popular Belgian beers, you will probably find me in the Hollandse Vismijn. This cheap and cheerful 'people's pub' is on the Fish Market. It is the type of café where everybody knows everybody and where you always get a warm welcome. Cheers!'

SHOPPING LIST

» **Antiquariaat Van de Wiele**, Sint-Salvatorskerkhof 7, tel. +32 (0)50 33 63 17, www.marcvandewiele.com

'For art and history, I was fortunate enough to discover Marc Van de Wiele Antiques. This is undoubtedly one of the best addresses in a city that is rich in antique shops. The place to find unique, illustrated books from days long gone by.'

» **Den Gouden Karpel**, Vismarkt 9-10-11, tel. +32 (0)50 33 33 89, www.dengoudenkarpel.be

'The fishing family Ameloot have been running Den Gouden Karpel with heart and soul for many years: not only an excellent catering service and fishmongers, but also a top-class fish bar, where you can enjoy the very best seafood (*fruits de mer*). For a fish-lover like myself, it is hard to walk past Den Gouden Karpel without stopping to buy something.'

» **Boekhandel De Reyghere**, Markt 12, tel. +32 (0)50 33 34 03, www.dereyghere.be
'For all my other reading material I rely on De Reyghere, located on the Market Square. Foreign visitors feel instantly at home in this book and newspaper store, primarily because of the large number of international titles it has on sale.'

» **D's Deldycke traiteurs**, Wollestraat 23, tel. +32 (0)50 33 43 35, www.deldycke.be
'In the 15th century, the Spaniard Pedro Tafur was already praising Bruges for its wide selection of exotic fruits and rare spices. The Deldycke caterer is proud to continue this centuries-old tradition. Here, all your culinary wishes will be fulfilled.'

» **Parallax**, Zuidzandstraat 17, tel. +32 (0)50 33 23 02, www.parallax.be
'I always buy my socks at Parallax, but they are also experts at stylishly camouflaging my beer belly! Highly recommended for other fashion victims and the vestimentally challenged! Boss, Scabal, Zilton, Falke: you can find them all here.'

SECRET TIP

» **Museumshop**, Hof Arents, Dijver 16, www.museabrugge.be
'Whoever enters the museum shop of the Groeninge Museum will surely leave with some wonderful memories. Perhaps you will take home your favourite art treasures in the shape of a handsomely illustrated book, a reproduction, a poster or picture postcard. And why don't you surprise yourself with an original Bruges gadget?'

» **Jerusalem Chapel**, **Gezelle Museum, Lace Centre**, **Church of Our Lady of the Pottery** and **Museum of Folk Life**: *see pages 54, 63, 66, 67-68 and 74 for more information.*

'Whenever I want to take a breather, I saunter down Saint Anne's, Bruges' most striking working-class neighbourhood. You can still sense the charm of an authentic community in the streets around the **Museum of Folk Life**. The area boasts many fascinating places, too. Off the cuff, if I may: Our Lady of the Pottery, the Lace Centre, the medieval Jerusalem Chapel and the Gezelle Museum.'

Bruges, international hotspot for classical music

Ayako Ito feels at home in the city where music is always in the air

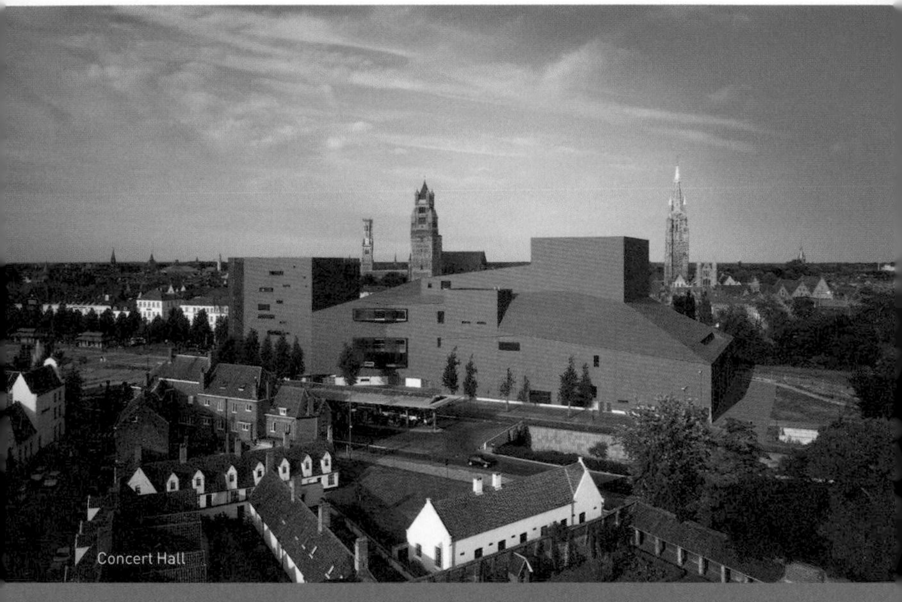

Concert Hall

It was written in the stars that Ayako Ito would one day end up in Bruges. After all, the world heritage city loves early music and so it was natural that it should immediately embrace the Japanese pianist, who specialises in playing the authentic pianoforte. What's more, in the city where music is always in the air, Ayako met a soulmate in Jos Van Immerseel.

ID-CARD

Name: Ayako Ito
Nationality: Japanese
Date of birth: 23 December
Born in Tokyo, moved to Antwerp in 1998 and settled in Bruges in 2017.

To say that the Japanese pianist Ayako Ito lives and breathes music is an understatement. Music guided her from distant Tokyo, via a stopover in Antwerp, to Bruges. Through that same music, she got to know her husband, the conductor and pianist Jos Van Immerseel. 'I came to Belgium as a pianist to learn the pianoforte – the 18th and 19th century piano – at the Antwerp Royal Conservatory. I was given the opportunity to practice on an instrument from 1826, an incredible privilege and something that is simply not possible in Japan. After four years, I obtained my Master's degree. Following that, I started teaching at the Antwerp Conservatory, but after a while I returned to Tokyo, taking with me two historical instruments that I had acquired during my stay in Belgium. This turned out not to be such a good idea. The Japanese climate is completely different, much more humid than here, which did my instruments no good at all. Those fantastic pianos just didn't sound right in Tokyo. Realising this, I decided to return to Belgium.' Ayako settled in Bruges, which, coincidently, is the home base of Anima Eterna Brugge, an international orchestra famed for its historically accurate performances on period instruments, which is conducted by Ayako's husband, Jos.

Maintaining and developing our musical heritage

Place and time seem to be of little importance to Ayako. The pianist feels at home on two continents and refuses to be confined to a single musical era. 'It's like I'm constantly time-travelling, which is a fantastic experience. In Tokyo, everything is brand-new, while in Bruges you realise that we are all a part of history. We receive things from the previous generation and we pass things on to the next generation.' In Bruges, all the puzzle pieces fell neatly into place for Ayako. 'Bruges is a historic city, a world heritage city. When I walk around here, I'm always impressed by the beautiful and precious things that people have managed to preserve. Here, early music is always in the air and it feels natural to play an original instrument in this setting. It's as if you belong to a greater whole. Not only do we try to preserve our musical heritage

'Anyone who performs well in the Concert Hall is certain to conquer the rest of the world.'

as best as we can, but we also try to develop and extend it. Early music and Bruges go hand in hand. It's something organic'. Ayako experiences daily the great love for early music that exists in Flanders. 'Music really lives here and there is a lot of interest in the kind of music we make. Of course, it helps that there are many unique initiatives and events: the MAfestival, for example, is world-famous. As a musician, you are used to people coming up to you for a chat after a concert, but in Bruges that happens on the street, in a restaurant, in a shop... It's almost as if the city supports us and carries us. We feel very much loved here as musicians, which is wonderful. It means that Bruges really is our city.'

Unforgettable, intense moments

The Concert Hall is an important factor in Bruges' love for music. It is the place where both musicians and music lovers can enjoy their passion and recharge their batteries. 'The Concert Hall is truly a top-tier international venue. It is a very special place: anyone who performs well here is certain to conquer the rest of the world. Not only is the Concert Hall blessed with excellent acoustics, it also has a warm, interested audience. And that makes us,

A FRESH VIEW ON 'BRUGES, CLASSICAL MUSIC CITY'

The famous Concert Hall is more than just a music temple for multi-day festivals, contemporary dance performances and top concerts. The Concertgebouw (Concert Hall) Circuit introduces you to Bruges as a classical music city in an original way. During an interactive experience route, you will learn about the famous acoustics of both the impressive main auditorium and the more intimate Chamber Music Hall. You will also explore the building's remarkable modern architecture and discover its surprising contemporary art collection. What's more, the route gives you the opportunity to be your own 'musician' at one of the many sound installations. The icing on the cake is a visit to the rooftop terrace on the seventh floor, where a stunning view over Bruges awaits you.

See page 60 for more practical information on the Concertgebouw Circuit.

5 X NOT-TO-BE-MISSED, ACCORDING TO AYAKO ITO

1. **Bach**'s enchanting **harpsichord concertos** (19/1/2019 – by the ***Akademie für Alte Musik Berlin***) are rarely performed. In these virtuoso and moving concertos, Bach goes beyond all previously known musical boundaries. *Read more about the Bach Academy Brugge, of which this concert is part, on page 78.*
2. Sixteen dancers from ***Rosas***, the world-renowned ensemble of Anne Teresa De Keersmaeker, interpret **the six Brandenburg concertos by J. S. Bach** (27 and 28/2/2019).
3. On 8/3/2019, ***Anima Eterna Brugge*** and ***baritone Thomas Bauer*** perform works by **Wolf, Mahler and Brahms**. The programme includes intimate chamber music and emotional love songs.
4. ***Les Muffatti***, directed by harpsichordist ***Bertrand Cuiller***, evoke the four elements – fire, air, water and earth – in an occasionally fierce, cosmic interpretation of several baroque dance suites (**The four elements**, 6/4/2019). *Read more about the Kosmos Festival, of which this performance is part, on page 79-80.*
5. On 16/5/2019, the ***Budapest Festival Orchestra*** plays **Mozart, Rossini & Schubert**. *Read more about the Budapest Festival on page 80.* *More info on www.concertgebouw.be.*

the musicians, want to give our best. If the audience is concentrated, we're that little bit sharper as well, which is how we take each other to a higher level.' This provides for unforgettable moments that leave a lasting impression on both musician and spectator alike. 'Making music makes me feel alive. I constantly communicate with the audience, I continuously exchange energy with them, and that is very intense. When everything fits perfectly, it's pure magic. And playing alongside my husband is even better. You create special moments together, making you fully aware that you are living intensely, with all your senses on fire.'

Ayako Ito's
best addresses

FAVOURITE SPOT

» **Concertgebouw**, 't Zand 34, tel. +32 (0)50 47 69 99, www.concertgebouw.be and www.concertgebouwcircuit.be

'The **Concert Hall**'s excellent reputation is fully justified. As a musician, this is the place where you give a lot but also receive a lot, thanks in no small measure to the perfect acoustics. The feeling of hearing what the audience hears is priceless. If you want to discover our Bruges music temple in an original way, Concertgebouw Circuit offers a varied experience route through the entire building. Otherwise, of course, you can always take in a concert or a dance performance.'

RESTAURANTS

» **Patrick Devos**, Zilverstraat 41, tel. +32 (0)50 33 55 66, www.patrickdevos.be

'I love to enter this centuries-old building with its authentic Art Nouveau and Art Deco lounges, where you can enjoy contemporary gastronomy at its best. Light, healthy and very bio. An exceptional place.'

» **Poules Moules**, Simon Stevinplein 9, tel. +32 (0)50 34 61 19, www.poulesmoules.be

'The place to be in Bruges for mussels, which is the specialty of the house. And if the weather permits, you can sit on the delightful terrace with its view of the Simon Stevinplein.'

» **Brasserie Raymond**, Eiermarkt 5, tel. +32 (0)50 33 78 48, www.brasserie-raymond.be

'This brasserie is a household name in Bruges. It serves excellent food in a classy setting: it's almost as if you step back into the past and star in your own movie!'

» **De Mangerie**, Oude Burg 20, tel. +32 (0)50 33 93 36, www.mangerie.com

'I love the original approach of De Mangerie, where the chef always knows how to surprise you with fantastic new creations. Here you can taste the passion for Eastern culture, fused astonishingly well with French cuisine.'

» **Refter**, Molenmeers 2, tel. +32 (0)50 44 49 00, www.bistrorefter.com

'Professional service, high-level gastronomy, a beautiful interior and a lovely terrace. In short, a great meal at a special location. What more could you ask?'

CAFÉS

» **Concertgebouwcafé**, 't Zand 34, tel. +32 (0)50 47 69 99, www.concertgebouw.be/en/concertgebouwcafe

'This really is our favourite place to take a breather before or after the concert. Ideal for a chat with the audience and our colleagues. A stimulating setting, but very cosy.

» **Brewery De Halve Maan**, Walplein 26, tel. +32 (0)50 44 42 22, www.halvemaan.be

'I like to visit this Bruges city brewery, which can boast a remarkable history. Nowadays, you find beers brewed by De Halve Maan all over the world; even Tokyo has its own Brugse Zot Café! It is also possible to give or watch concerts in the brewery buildings. Relaxing to music with a beer in your hand: what could be better? '

» **De Verloren Hoek**, Carmersstraat 178, tel. +32 (0)50 69 80 19, www.deverlorenhoek.be

'This very cosy bistro is situated just around the corner from where we live. To me, De Verloren Hoek means friendly staff and dishes with an original twist. The beautiful view of the ramparts and the windmills comes free of charge.'

» **Le Pain Quotidien**, Simon Stevinplein 15, tel. +32 (0)50 34 29 21, www.lepainquotidien.be

'I'm a big fan of Le Pain Quotidien. Its concept is fantastic: when you sit down at one of the large tables, you almost immediately start up a spontaneous conversation with your neighbours! The food is prepared with great care and is delicious. The terrace is highly recommended as well.'

» **Bar Jus**, Kleine Sint-Amandsstraat 10, tel. +32 (0)50 61 32 77, www.bar-jus.be
'Bar Jus is a bit off the beaten track, but well worth the effort to find it. Here you can sample a fine selection of outstanding wines, which can be ordered by the glass. It's always nice to discover something new. And while you sip the heavenly nectar, you can watch the world go by on the street.'

SHOPPING LIST

» **Rombaux**, Mallebergplaats 13, tel. +32 (0)50 33 25 75, www.rombaux.be

'This fantastic music store is already a hundred years old. Building up a tradition of this kind is only possible if you offer nothing but the best. Here you can flick through music scores, handle and test new instruments, meet other musicians ... reasons enough not to buy online.'

» **Villa Maria**, Gistelse Steenweg 18-28, tel. +32 (0)50 31 07 44, www.villamaria.be
'In this delightful boutique you will find the latest collections of many leading fashion brands. Whenever I'm in urgent need of a new outfit, I head straight for Villa Maria. I know I'll always leave with something elegant and stylish.'

» **lilola shop**, Langestraat 47b-49, tel. +32 (0)50 33 66 02, www.lilola.be

'Here you can find lots of outfits and accessories, not only from international brands, but also from up-and-coming talent. Everything I buy here is perfect to wear for either a concert or a party. And on top of that, you get their reliable advice for free.'

» **Frederiek Van Pamel**, Ezelstraat 33, tel. +32 (0)50 34 44 80, www.frederiekvanpamel.be

'Entering Frederiek's store is like entering another world. It is a wonderful place that combines interior design with flowers. Exotic, highly colourful and very stylish.'

» **The Chocolate Line**, Simon Stevinsplein 19, tel. +32 (0)50 34 10 90, www.thechocolateline.be

'Each time I leave for Japan, I first call in at The Chocolate Line, so that I can surprise my friends and family with the contemporary and original pralines for which the shop is rightly famous. Dominique Persoone's chocolate creations are so tasty you can hardly keep your hands off them!'

SECRET TIP

» **Chapel of Our Lady of the Blind**, Kreupelenstraat 8, tel. +32 (0)50 32 76 60 or +32 (0)50 33 68 41, www.brugsebelofte.be

'The history of this beautiful **chapel** dates back to 1305. Originally built by Robert of Béthune to commemorate the Battle of Pevelenberg, a battle fought between Flanders and France, it truly is a hidden gem. I only discovered it because I was once asked to perform here. In the 15th century, **seven small houses** were built next to the chapel to offer shelter to the blind people of the city. A special place that you really must visit.'

Inspirational makers in Bruges
Creative jack-of-all-trades Djamil Zenasni on timeless craftsmanship

Djamil Zenasni

Many people do the same job all their lives. Others are much too curious to contemplate anything of the kind. All-round craftsman Djamil Zenasni belongs to the latter category. Renovating houses, making ceramic pottery, upholstering furniture: he does it all, and all with the same passion and enthusiasm. So let's meet this remarkable man, who is helping to continue Bruges' centuries-old tradition for craftsmanship of the highest quality.

ID-CARD

Name: Djamil Zenasni
Nationality: Belgian
Date of birth: 27 November 1963
Born in Oran (Algeria), came first to Brussels via France, but has been living in Bruges since 1985.

Djamil Zenasni is blessed with an inborn curiosity. What's more, he has used this special characteristic to map out for himself an interesting but unorthodox pathway through life. A pathway, at least in career terms, which has been unusual right from the very start. Having secured his university degree in economics, he went to work as... a partner in a cheese-making factory based exclusively on traditional methods in Ghent. 'It was a small co-operative, where I learnt a great deal: not only how to speak Dutch, but also about the value of an ecological approach and the importance of slow food.'

Versatile and creative

When Djamil's wife found a job in Ostend, the young couple went in

'If you do something with passion and concentration, then the rest of the world just disappears and you are absorbed in the enjoyment of the moment. That's a wonderful feeling.'

#LOCALLOVE – A FINE SELECTION OF AUTHENTIC SHOPS

With the #LocalLove city map in your hand, you can discover a fine selection of Bruges shopping addresses with character. No mass production here, but specialist businesses spread across the city, each offering top quality and each run for more than five years by a passionate local entrepreneur or a creative Bruges craftsperson. Their specialities are many and varied: delicatessen shops, interior design, original fashion stores, rare books and manuscripts... If you are looking for something a little bit out of the ordinary and are prepared to leave the beaten track to find it, shopping in shops where the locals also love to go, then the #LocalLove addresses are ideal for you. Sounds like your cup of tea? Pick up a free #LocalLove map from one of the i tourist offices.

For more shopping pleasure, also take a look at pages 87-89 and page 130.

CRAFTSMANSHIP IN BRUGES, A CENTURIES-OLD HISTORY!

In the Middle Ages, the craftsmen came together in guilds to defend their interests. These guilds were also politically active, something that in Bruges was codified in the city charter dating from the second half of the 13th century. There were some 50 recognized trades, a number that remained stable for centuries. Masons, smiths, cabinet makers, bakers, butchers, thatchers, tilers, tanners, furriers and silversmiths, but also the makers of rosaries and weapons. These were all trades performed by hand and for which a certain period of training and apprenticeship was required. Each trade was subject to a number of very strict provisions to ensure the quality of the finished products. For example, the cobblers in Bruges were only allowed to make shoes from new leather. Similarly, carpenters were forbidden to work at night, whereas woodcarvers could, but only if a foreign merchant was waiting urgently for one of their statues. Even today, it is still possible to spot some of the old guild halls in the city's streets; for example, on the Steenstraat (no. 25, 38 and 40) and the Huidenvettersplein (no.10). These fine buildings underline the power and prestige the guilds once enjoyed. But even today, Bruges still sets great store by the value of craftsmanship.

Read more on page 87 about the skill and passion of Bruges' 21st century artisans.

search of a house – and a neighbourhood – where they could feel at home. They eventually ended up in Bruges, where they lost their hearts to a residence near the Queen Astrid Park, which was large enough to open a B&B. However, the building first needed quite a lot of improvement and to keep down costs Djamil did most of the work himself. He soon realized that he was quite good at – and quite liked – working with his hands: carpentry, electrical installation, plumbing: he learnt it all and did it all. In the meantime, he also became fascinated by the idea of making artisanal footstools with natural fibres. 'After that, I began upholstering chairs as well, and was soon making new wooden legs for them. One thing led to another. The armchair collection was something that developed organically.'

Always giving the best of yourself

As the years passed, Djamil used his budding skills to transform house after house. He restored them from cellar to attic, and often then filled them with his own self-made furniture. The houses might vary in size and style, but there was always one constant: Djamil devoted himself to their renovation with his typically southern enthusiasm and the end results invariably displayed the same good taste and a distinctive fresh approach. 'You've always got to start again from scratch, do it as though you are do-

ing it for the very first time. That's the only way to avoid repeating yourself. Every project is new. Every house is different. You've got to begin each time with a blank page. In that way, you keep on learning.' Yet even though Djamil seems to be constantly reinventing himself, his style is immediately recognizable: bold, warm colours, authentic materials and an eclectic mix of furniture.
His own shop, at Hoogstraat 42, reflects the different aspects of Djamil's many talents. You can find a handful of his handmade footstools and chairs – each one a unique piece – and also a number of colourful ceramics, his latest passion. 'Many visitors, intrigued by all the colours, curiously come inside. Until recently, I always had to disappoint them. I had very few small things in the shop and you can hardly take home a piece of furniture in your suitcase!' And so Djamil decided to develop his own hand-made collection of robust yet elegant sugar pots, salad bowls, etc., which you can now find stacked in neat piles in his store.

Passions for life

For outsiders, it might seem as though this multi-talented craftsman flits restlessly from one project to another. But that's not true. 'I have a lot of interests and I like to know everything about them. What I do, I do with my whole heart. Not just for six months, but for the rest of my life.' Djamil regards all his skills equally. 'If you do something with passion and concentration, then the rest of the world just disappears and you are

absorbed in the enjoyment of the moment. That's a wonderful feeling.'
He is not too bothered about expanding his ceramics career and does not dream about becoming an export success. 'That's something I learnt at the cheese factory. Bigger isn't necessarily better. Small and healthy – you don't need any more than that. And I see that many of my craftsmen-colleagues feel the same. In recent years the shopping climate has changed. It's not only visitors but also local people who now want authentic products. They are happy to search for them in the side streets, away from the well-known shopping circuits. I can see a growing interest for specialist stores, neighbourhood shops, local trade. Not just here in the Hoogstraat and the Langestraat, but also, for example, in the Smedenstraat, where there are lots of shops within easy walking distance where you can do your daily shopping. I think it's the personal service you get in these shops that most appeals to people. And for us shopkeepers, what can be better than to have satisfied customers?'

Djamil Zenasni's **best addresses**

FAVOURITE SPOT

» **Minneboplein**
'It was thanks to the work *Lanchals* by John Powers, which graced the **Minneboplein** during the 2018 Triennial, that I rediscovered this wonderful place. Although it is by no means hidden, I had walked past it dozens of times without noticing. A small, restful corner along the canals, where you can find a bit of peace and quiet.'

RESTAURANTS

» **Lieven**, Philipstockstraat 45, tel. +32 (0)50 68 09 75, www.etenbijlieven.be
'Lieven is my neighbour and we say hello to each other every day. For special occasions we have a night out at his elegant restaurant, so that we can celebrate in style. Top-level enjoyment!'

» **Sud**, Mallebergplaats 5, tel. +32 (0)50 34 45 62, www.sudinbrugge.com
'Here you can eat pure Italian cuisine from Puglia, simple but deliciously prepared. You can either eat it on site or else take it home to enjoy. Ideal for whoever doesn't feel like cooking! And if they are holding a special party, they often come for some of my hand-made bowls. A perfect combo!'

» **Carlito's**, Hoogstraat 21, tel. +32 (0)50 49 00 75, www.carlitos.be
'The best pizzas in town. And all served up in a trendy decor that is also child-friendly.'

» **Duc de Bourgogne**, Huidenvettersplein 12, tel. +32 (0)50 33 20 38, www.ducdebourgogne.be

'Certainly the most beautifully situated restaurant in Bruges. Grandeur from the days of yesteryear, with silver cutlery and a magnificent view over the canals. Go there for lunch and ask for a table by the water.'

» **Sint-Joris**, Markt 29, tel. +32 (0)50 33 30 62, www.restaurant-sintjoris.be

'When the son of an organic farmer runs a restaurant, you can be sure that the meat will be home-grown, healthy and top quality. That's what makes this such a great address. And right on the market square!'

CAFÉS

» **Craenenburg**, Markt 16, tel. +32 (0)50 33 34 02, www.craenenburg.be

'Huis Craenenburg has occupied a prominent place in Bruges' history for centuries. Today, locals come to this grand café to read the newspaper and exchange gossip. It is also where the carriage drivers come for their early morning coffee before setting off for their day's work. This is a place you don't want to miss. Friendly and reliable.'

» **Coffeebar Adriaan**, Adriaan Willaertstraat 7, tel. +32 (0)476 90 13 10, www.coffeebaradriaan.be

'A perfect espresso in the stately setting of an old bank building. That's Adriaan's! Enjoying your coffee in style.'

» **Comptoir des Arts**, Vlamingstraat 53, tel. +32 (0)494 38 79 61, www.comptoirdesarts.be

'Beer and blues in an old-world cellar café. To add to the ambiance, they regularly host live music and comedy evenings.'

» **Café Vlissinghe**, Blekersstraat 2, tel. +32 (0)50 34 37 37, www.cafevlissinghe.be
'The oldest tavern in Bruges and an institution in its own right. A place where it seems as though time has stood still. In the heart of the city, but with a fine garden and pétanque court.'

» **Riesling & Pinot Winebar-Wineshop**, Hoogstraat 33, tel. +32 (0)50 84 23 97, www.riesling-pinot.be
'Here, just around the corner from my place, I like to come and enjoy a good glass of wine and a bite to eat. Not so long ago I knew nothing about German wine, but now I've been converted into a firm believer!'

SHOPPING LIST

» **Depot d'O**, Ridderstraat 21, tel. +32 (0)495 23 65 95, www.depotdo.be
'I make most things for myself. But if there is something 'extra' I need, then I know that Kurt's is the place to look. Depot d'O is the address for lovers of vintage design and quirky bits and pieces. If you can think of it, you can probably find it here.'

» **Galerie Thomas Serruys**, Keersstraat 2, tel. +32 (0)477 92 43 68, www.thomasserruys.com
'Are you looking for that once-in-a-lifetime piece of vintage design you know you've got to have as soon as you see it? You are? Then Thomas Serruys is guaranteed to have it. A store that knows precisely what makes things timeless – and irresistible.'

» **Maud Bekaert**, Sint-Clarastraat 40, tel. +32 (0)475 26 95 58, www.maudbekaert.be
'To call Maud Bekaert a letter-cutter is to do her an injustice. This outwardly frail-looking young craftswoman wields her hammer and chisel with a remarkable firmness and flexibility, creating wonderfully sculpted calligraphy in natural stone, concrete and metal. This is the place to come if you want a really super-original present.'

» **Patisserie Academie**, Vlamingstraat 56, tel. +32 (0)50 68 92 91, www.patisserieacademie.be

'Tom Van Loock learnt his patisserie skills in De Karmeliet, a former star-rated restaurant. After a few years, he opened his own shop, a pure pleasure temple where only perfection is good enough. His cakes are so delicious that you want to eat them as soon as you are back on the street! Tom swears by traditional methods and a personal approach – and you can taste it in the end product.'

» **Quicke**, Zuidzandstraat 21-23, tel. +32 (0)50 33 23 00, www.quicke.be

'Quicke has been a byword for fashion in Bruges for more than 118 years, but also attracts fashionistas from all over the world. And with good reason. Its top-quality shoes and bags are always well ahead of the trends and last for years and years without losing any of their elegant refinement. A store for ladies who want to score.'

SECRET TIP

» **Groenerei**

'The back gable of my shop looks out over the supremely beautiful **Groenerei** canal. Since recently, this wall has been graced by a mural painting of a dancing couple, my nodding tribute to the Flemish Expressionists, because I sometimes think that I'm a bit of Flemish Expressionist myself! If you are walking along the Groenerei you will need to look carefully to see it – but seek and ye shall find!'

In search of artistic treasures and inspirational places

Mirna Hidalgo finds creativity in a city with a heart for art

Jean Moust

Flamenco dancer, expert in international law, creative coach and ... artist, a graduate from the Bruges Academy, no less! The Argentinean Mirna Hidalgo has always seized life's opportunities with both hands, but it was only in her new hometown of Bruges that she finally found her way into the world of the fine arts. A story about love and creativity.

ID-CARD

Name: Mirna Hidalgo
Nationality: Belgian
Date of birth: 11 July 1966
Born and raised in Argentina, but led by love to Bruges.

There are people who seem able to succeed effortlessly in five or six different lives. Mirna Hidalgo is just this kind of multi-talented busy bee. By the time she was 20, she was a professional flamenco dancer. In between all her other activities, she also obtained a law degree. After graduating, Mirna decided to spend a relaxing summer travelling across Europe by train. In Paris, on the eve of her return to Argentina, someone told her that no trip to Europe was complete without a visit to the beautiful city of Bruges. And so she made her way to Bruges, where on her very first evening she got talking to a local who was keen to practice his Spanish. Some months later, after the exchange of several letters, this man from Bruges took a plane to Buenos Aires and at the end of his holiday Dirk asked Mirna to marry him. Mirna said 'yes'. Dirk went home to make all the necessary arrangements, returning a couple of months later when everything had been completed. 'A day after his arrival back in Argentina we were married. If you know something is good, there is no reason to doubt or hesitate. In the meantime, we have been married for 30 years and are still very much in love.'

Learning from the best

And so it was that the 23-year-old Mirna arrived in Bruges. She learnt Dutch and French and decided to extend her academic studies by following a course in international law. After that, she spent 20 years successfully pursuing a career in the world of high finance, although in the meantime she continued to broaden her range of talents through further study, especially in the fields of psychology and coaching. 'Over the years, I have come to understand that curiosity is my main driving force. If I stand still, I soon get bored.'
There came a point, however, when her work consisted of nothing more than making constant cuts and savings. 'That's nothing for me. I need a job with more creativity.' Mirna decided that she

'Bruges is an amazingly beautiful city and everyone who lives here is aware of the privilege.'

needed a career switch. 'I had never painted before but one day in the supermarket I saw a special offer on canvas and some paints. And so I bought them. That's how I started.'

Some people would be happy to start off slowly. But not Mirna. She immediately registered with the Bruges Academy of Fine Arts! 'I must admit that I did hesitate before taking such a bold step. This was not just any old course. The Bruges Academy is the oldest in Flanders and has been around for more than 300 years. It was founded in the 18th century in the Burghers' Lodge on the Jan van Eyck square and the collection of paintings they built up later went on to form the basis for the Groeninge Museum, the museum of fine arts in Bruges. In other words, it is a great privilege to be allowed to be a part of the Academy's story. Many masters with international reputations first started their artistic careers here. The idea that I could learn from them and help to further that same tradition made me humble and very grateful. At the end of the 19th century, the Academy donated its collection to the city, which prompted the local authorities to build a brand-new museum to house it. This is the Groeninge Museum, which you can find on the Dijver. Which just happens to be in the part of town that also has some of my favourite art and antique shops! Talk about a happy coincidence!'

Everyone is creative

Mirna finds inspiration almost everywhere, which is why she always likes to keep her eyes open as she makes her way through the city. 'Each week I cycle to the Academy and each ride along the old ramparts is different. That has an inspirational effect. You can see the seasons and the light changing. Bruges is an amazingly beautiful city and everyone who lives here is aware of the privilege.' Coaching and art may seem like two very different worlds, but Mirna not only manages to combine them but even to

FIND YOUR OWN ART TREASURES WITH #ARTANDANTIQUES

#ArtandAntiques
VISIT BRUGES

For lovers of centuries-old objéts d'art, unique manuscripts, 17th century paintings, more modern artistic creations and contemporary photography, Bruges is a veritable paradise – and not just in the city's museums! Let the #ArtandAntiques map lead you to some of the finest and most reputable art galleries and antique stores, where you can make your acquaintance with the unique and high-quality offer that has something to suit every taste and budget. So why not pop in to one of our i tourist offices and pick up a free copy of the #Artand Antiques map. *For more addresses you really don't want to miss, it is also worth taking a look at pages 87-89 and 121.*

DISCOVER THE WORKS OF ART THAT MOVE AND INSPIRE MIRNA HIDALGO

1. In the pharmacy garden of the centuries-old St. John's Hospital stands ***Pax*** by Octave Rotsaert, who was once a teacher at the Bruges Academy. This intimate statue expresses a passionate desire for world peace.
2. With his ***Horsemen of the Apocalypse*** Rik Poot shows us in the idyllic setting of the Hof Arents garden the sufferings and shortcomings of mankind.
3. In 1489, Hans Memling completed his unbelievably detailed ***St. Ursula Shrine***, which was commissioned by the St. John's Hospital and is still on display at the location for which it was created.
4. At the Steenhouwersdijk there is a bronze version of Constant Permeke's ***Niobe***. The petrified tears of this mother of seven sons and seven daughters – all fourteen of whom were killed – flow here, as it were, into the river Reie.
5. My favourite work in the St. Anne's Church is Hendrik Herregouts' ***Last Judgement***. It's a good idea to first walk all the way to the altar and only then turn around to look at the painting: you will be amazed by what you see!

merge them into one. 'Dealing with people is also pure creativity. You make a connection with the other person and every following step in the relationship is based on that connection. Together, you construct something, something that is always unique. Once I organized a series of events where every participant had to make a painting in just two hours. And it worked, because everyone is creative. It's just that nowadays most people no longer realize it. When the participants put down their brushes, we all walked around the room together to see what everyone had painted. The result in each case was something individual and unique. This is tremendously empowering. No matter who you are, you are valuable.'

Mirna Hidalgo's **best addresses**

FAVOURITE SPOT

» **St. Magdalene's Church**, at the corner of the Stalijzerstraat and the Schaarstraat, www.yot.be

'This church is anything but ordinary. From the outside, it might look like a simple, standard Neo-Gothic building, but inside it is the most **wonderful place to sit and reflect**. The modern style of decoration is surprising, with a peaceful water feature, swing and bright colours. And the more you look around, the more you discover. What's more, the church often hosts interesting exhibitions of different kinds.'

RESTAURANTS

» **Bistro Zwart Huis**, Kuipersstraat 23, tel. +32 (0)50 69 11 40, www.bistrozwarthuis.be

'If you are looking for a little culinary pampering, you could do much worse than try Bistro Zwart Huis, with its monumental banqueting room in a listed building dating from 1482. Here classic Flemish dishes are served alongside a fine selection of world cuisine. The bistro also regularly hosts blues or jazz concerts, which makes your dining experience complete!'

» **Malesherbes**, Stoofstraat 3-5, tel. +32 (0)50 33 69 24

'You can find this excellent restaurant in one of the narrowest streets in Bruges. Its hallmarks are honest, fresh products and French-style cuisine: the chef learnt his trade from a celebrated French cook. We celebrate our wedding anniversary each year in Malesherbes. We love its warm and personal approach.'

» **Passion For Food**, Philipstockstraat 39, tel. +32 (0)477 40 17 14
'A limited menu, but each dish is healthy and delicious. The restaurant offers both veggie and vegan options. The super-friendly owner, Sherif, knows almost everything there is to know about Bruges and is a perfect host.'

» **Ventura Ristorante**, Koningin Elisabethlaan 48A, tel. +32 (0)50 69 39 74 or +32 (0)477 89 57 46, www.venturaristorante.be
'Ventura only opened its doors recently, but is already one of our favourites. Here you can eat authentic Italian cooking at its best. It's another great place to go when you have something to celebrate.'

» **Petite Aneth**, Maria van Bourgondiëlaan 1, tel. +32 (0)50 31 11 89, www.aneth.be
'Yet another of our festive favourites. For many years the chef ran a star-rated restaurant, but is still producing equally great food in this more modest establishment. Fine gastronomy at a reasonable price.'

CAFÉS

» **27Bflat**, Katelijnestraat 27B, tel. +32 (0)479 29 74 29, www.27bflat.be
'If you don't know it's there, you can easily walk past this place without noticing it. Which would be a shame. Because behind its inconspicuous door there is a vibrant cafe, complete with its own sunny garden. Live jazz music adds the perfect finishing touch.'

» **Cuvee QV Winebar/Wineshop**, Philipstockstraat 41, tel. +32 (0)50 33 33 28, www.cuvee.be
'This establishment only serves and sells top-quality wines, the kind of bottles you won't find in your local supermarket. Not cheap, perhaps, but it gives you the chance to sample fine wines before you are sure you want to splash out on a few bottles for your cellar. And even if you aren't planning to buy in bulk, it's a super place to come for just a refreshing glass – or maybe two.'

» **Blend Winebar-Wineshop**, Kuipersstraat 6-8, tel. +32 (0)497 17 20 85, www.uncorked.be

'Blend also offers a wide selection of wines that is regularly updated. Here you can drink good vintages from every price category, while the range of snacks and tit-bits make sure that your head stays cool...'

» **Lucifernum**, Twijnstraat 6, tel. +32 (0)476 35 06 51, www.lucifernum.be

'This is the odd-one-out in my address list. It's not always open and you need to pay an admission fee. But it's well worth the money, because once inside you will be find yourself in a crazy world full of art, with one of the most beautiful garden terraces in all Bruges. Truly an experience not to be missed.'

» **Tonka**, Walplein 18, tel. +32 (0)495 20 73 99, www.tonkatearoom.com

'A small tearoom run by a young couple who really put their heart and soul into it. The pancakes are fresh-made *à la minute* and their delicious quiche is served with a crisp salad and a croissant straight from the oven.'

SHOPPING LIST

» **Absolute Art Gallery**, Dijver 4-5, tel. +32 (0)50 49 10 12, www.absoluteartgallery.com

'To keep my finger on the pulse of what is happening on the international art scene, I frequently call in at the Absolute Art Gallery. You are always guaranteed a warm welcome and can learn more about the recent work of leading international artists. In particular, I am always charmed by the restful landscapes of Benoît Trimborn.'

» **Galerie Pinsart**, Genthof 21, tel. +32 (0)50 67 50 66, www.pinsart.be

'Pinsart always seem to have new and interesting contemporary exhibitions. As a result, it's well worth popping in on a regular basis. I enjoy just wandering around this beautifully converted 18th century building, admiring all its wonderful works of art.'

» **De Schacht**, Katelijnestraat 49, tel. +32 (0)50 33 44 24, www.de-schacht.be
'This is *my* art shop, conveniently located just a stone's throw from the Academy. A paradise for anyone who is creative, but also a great place to find original presents that will please even the less creative souls among your acquaintances.'

» **Kunsthandel Pollentier-Maréchal**, Sint-Salvatorskerkhof 8, tel. +32 (0)50 33 18 04, www.pollentier-marechal.be
'For lovers of prints and engravings, there is only one place in Bruges to go: Geert and Martine's shop, in the shadow of the St. Saviour's Cathedral. It is also the best address in town for all your framing, cleaning and restoration requirements. What's more, it still possesses the authentic charm of the old print cabinets of yesteryear. Wonderful.'

» **Jean Moust**, Mariastraat 15, tel. +32 (0)50 34 44 35, www.jeanmoust.com
'I am certainly no expert, but I am always moved to silence whenever I pass Jean Moust's gallery, with its dozens of Dutch and Flemish paintings from the 17th century. The blood-red walls are filled with a truly impressive collection of masterpieces. You hardly know where to look first. An overwhelming experience!'

SECRET TIP

» **The gardens of the Spanoghe almshouse**, Katelijnestraat 8
'It takes a little courage to keep on going, because at first it seems like one of those places where you shouldn't really be. But if you press on you will be rewarded with a perfect haven of peace and tranquillity, just metres from all the hustle and bustle of the busy city. It is a **marvellous spot to relax** for a few minutes, looking across the smooth **waters of the canal**. It also gives you an otherwise seldom seen view of the side gable of the St. John's Hospital and its adjoining convent.'

Lissewege

Discoveries outside of **Bruges**

The other Flemish historical cities

Antwerp (Antwerpen) 82 km

Antwerp has a lot to offer: a beautiful cathedral and numerous imposing churches, a magnificent Central Station, the ground-breaking Museum on the River (MAS), the tranquil Rubens House, a delightful sculpture garden (Middelheim), a zoo with a history and so much more. Antwerp is also Belgium's fashion capital, home to many internationally renowned designers. That is why in the Scheldt city you will find dozens of exclusive boutiques, rubbing shoulders with fun bric-a-brac shops where you can browse for hours! Not surprisingly, the local 'Antwerpenaars' – who are fairly loud by nature – are extremely proud of their city.

INFO > www.visitantwerpen.be; there is a direct train connection between Bruges and Antwerp (journey time: ca. 1.30 hours; www.belgiantrain.be).

Brussels (Brussel) 88 km

The whole world comes together in Brussels, with a different continent around every corner, from the exotic Matonge quarter to the stately elegance of the European institutions. The capital of Belgium has a vibrancy like no other and the formality of its 'hard' metropolitan structure is softened by the authentic, working-class ambiance of its more popular districts. In the shadow of the majestic Market Square, *Manneken-Pis* is permanently peeing. This diverse city reconciles the chic sophistication of the Zavel with the folksy informality of the Vossenplein. Royalty watchers rush eagerly to the Paleizenplein, art lovers can do their thing at one of the more than hundred museums and galleries, such as the Magritte Museum, the BOZAR (Museum of Fine Arts) or the Horta Museum. Foodies hurry to the numerous

food temples and gastronomic restaurants. Vintage-lovers climb to the top of the Atomium. And in the city where both Tintin and the Smurfs were born, comic lovers will find more than 50 comic-strip walls and a renowned Comics Museum.
INFO > www.visit.brussels; there is a direct train connection between Bruges and Bruxelles-Central (Brussels-Central, journey time: ca. 1.00-1.15 hours; www.belgiantrain.be).

Damme 6 km

Until the silting up of the tidal inlet Zwin, Damme was the transhipment port of Bruges. To reach the literary home of Tijl Uilenspiegel (Owlglass), you drive straight along the banks of the Damse Vaart (Damme Canal), one of the most beautiful pieces of nature in all Belgium. The canal is lined with magnificent poplars, some of which are over 100 years old. Their wind twisted trunks add to the charm of the setting. You can also experience their beauty from the water. The nostalgic paddle steamer *Lamme Goedzak* travels to and fro between the small medieval town and Bruges' Noorweegse Kaai (Norwegian Quay). And every second Sunday of the month, Damme is transformed into one big book centre!
INFO > www.visitdamme.be; scheduled bus no. 43 (not on Saturdays, Sundays and public holidays, see www.delijn.be for the time schedule), bus stop: Damme Plaats; or by the paddle steamer Lamme Goedzak, www.bootdamme-brugge.be *(for more information see page 51)*. You can also easily cycle to

Damme *(for bicycle rental see pages 154-155)* or hire a scooter to ride there *(see page 158 for scooter rental)*.

Ghent (Gent) 39 km

The people of Ghent have always been a bit rebellious. It's in their genes. They rose in revolt against Emperor Charles. As punishment, he made them walk through the streets with nooses around their necks. Ever since they have been known as 'noose wearers', a name they wear with pride. In Ghent you can find the medieval alongside the trendy. The centuries-old Belfry stands majestically alongside the new City Hall. The picturesque Patershol district, with its narrow streets and fun restaurants, stands in the shadow of the imposing Gravensteen Castle. The city is creating an international gastronomic furore with its young star-rated chefs and as the veggie capital of Europe. Art-lovers will find their way to the world-famous *The Adoration of the Mystic Lamb* by the van Eyck brothers in St. Bavo's Cathedral or one of the many museums. The S.M.A.K. (contemporary art), the Design Museum, the MSK (fine arts) and the STAM (city museum) will surprise you each season with top-class

exhibitions. The festivals, cultural events and vibrant night life guarantee non-stop fun and ambiance in the student city. And when the sun goes down, the Light Plan comes into its own. Buildings, squares and streets are bathed in atmospheric light. The ideal moment to visit local people's favourite place: the Graslei and the Korenlei alongside the quiet waters of the River Schelde.
INFO > www.visitgent.be; there is a direct train connection between Bruges and Ghent (Sint-Pieters) (journey time: ca. 30 min.; www.belgiantrain.be). Tram 1 rides from Ghent-Sint-Pieters railway station to the city centre every 10 minutes.

Louvain (Leuven) 110 km

Louvain is without a doubt the number one student city in Belgium. Dozens of historic university buildings are spread all over the old city centre. Leuven can proudly boast the largest and oldest university in Belgium, founded as long ago as 1425. Notwithstanding its long history, Leuven is always open to innovation, as can be seen in several remarkable architectural projects, such as the Stuk Art Centre, Het Depot, De Hoorn (The Horn) in the trendy Vaartkom district and the M-Museum Leuven. And then there is Louvain, city of beer. With two breweries – the giant Stella Artois plant and the smaller, more local Domus brewery – located in the city centre and with several other traditional brewers nearby, there is no excuse not to relax for a few moments with a foaming pint. And what better place than on the Oude Markt (Old Market), possibly the world's longest bar...
INFO > www.visitleuven.be; there is a direct train connection between Bruges and Leuven (journey time: ca. 1.30 to 1.40 hours; www.belgiantrain.be).

Malines (Mechelen) 90 km

Although the smallest of the Flemish art cities, Mechelen is well worth a visit. Exactly halfway between Antwerp and Brussels, Mechelen is more compact than its larger neighbours, but is equally well endowed with historical monuments and listed buildings, which allow you to relive the glory years of the Burgundian empire. The most well-known landmark is the proud St. Rombout's Cathedral. Its 97-metre high tower contains two sets of bells, which are regularly played by pupils of the Royal carillon school – the oldest and largest in the

world. It is also well worth paying a visit to the brand-new Hof van Busleyden, which brings Mechelen's rich history under Margaret of Austria to life. In addition, the River Dijle meanders through the city, enclosed by the Zoutwerf (Salt Quay) with its 16th century wooden frontages and the Haverwerf (Oat Quay) with its pastel-coloured decorative facades. Another 'must' is the former palace of Margaret of Austria, from where the Low Countries were once ruled. In short, everyone who visits Mechelen will discover a historic city bursting with contemporary charm and conviviality.

INFO > www.visitmechelen.be; there is a train connection between Bruges and Malines, with a single change of trains in Gent-Sint-Pieters or Bruxelles-Midi (Brussels-South) (journey time: ca. 1.30-1.45 hours; www.belgiantrain.be).

Ypres (Ieper) 46 km

Thanks to its flourishing cloth industry, Ypres, along with Bruges and Ghent, was one of the most powerful cities in Flanders in the 13th century. Its strategically important position in the Westhoek meant that the city was besieged on several occasions, resulting in the construction of strong defensive ramparts, which were further extended in the 17th century. Ypres also paid a heavy price during the First World War, when it was the scene of fierce fighting that left the city in ruins. It was rebuilt after the Armistice, and the most important buildings are exact copies of the originals, like the famous Cloth Hall. This magnificent building is also home to the In Flanders Fields Museum. Witnesses of the war tell their personal stories: these little histories reveal the huge emotions that are so sadly typical of all conflicts. This allows you to experience the horror of the trenches and the bombardment of the city. In the same building you can also find the Yper Museum, which introduces you to other aspects of the city's thousand-year-old history. Various (day) trips are organized from Bruges to Ypres and other sites of interest in the Westhoek *(see pages 146-147)*.

INFO > www.toerisme-ieper.be; there is a train connection between Bruges and Ypres, with a single change of trains in Courtrai (journey time: ca. 1.30 to 1.40 hours; www.belgiantrain.be); from Ypres station, it is approximately a 10-minute walk to the main Market Square.

Bruges' wood- and wetlands

The Bruges' wood- and wetlands form a green belt around the city. Here time passes more slowly and living the good life is all that counts. There are several star-rated chefs in the area, as well as numerous passionate regional producers. Add to this the picturesque canals that criss-cross the region, the flat polders that are a paradise for cyclists and the many historical buildings surrounded by lush greenery, and you can soon see why the Ommeland is a place that will live long in your memory. The world heritage city of Bruges is the beating heart of the region; the nostalgic towns and villages that surround it are its soul. Burgundian strolls through romantic castles, soaking up the history in Damme, Lissewege or one of the other timeless villages: anything goes, but there are no 'musts'. Everything is chill. Perhaps it's time to recharge your batteries and enjoy the delights of the Bruges Ommeland to the full!

INFO > www.brugseommeland.be

Damme

GUIDED TOURS THROUGH BRUGES' WOOD- AND WETLANDS

Nothing is quite so much fun as discovering the area of the wood- and wetlands around Bruges – known locally as Brugse Ommeland – with a guided tour. Bike-lovers can choose between the more energetic explorations of The Green Bike Tour (arlando@telenet.be), Pink Bear Bike Tours (www.pinkbear.be), Steershop biketours (www.steershop.be) or QuasiMundo Biketours Brugge (www.quasimundo.eu). Those who prefer a more relaxed approach can opt for the enjoyable 'Triple Treat: the best of Belgium in one day', a minibus tour by Quasimodo Tours (www.quasimodo.be).

TIP

The ideal way to discover the surroundings of Bruges is by bike. Enjoy nature to the full in the Bulskampveld Landscape Park, the most wooded area in West Flanders, or in the magnificent former castle estates of the public domains at Tillegem, Tudor and Beisbroek. And don't worry about getting lost: with a cycling network map in your hand, you can create your own easy-to-follow route. You can buy cycle routes in the i tourist offices or on shop.westtoer.be (See pages 154-155 for bicycle rental)

Not to be missed

The Uilenspiegel Museum (Damme, 6 km, www.visitdamme.be), the home of Tijl Uilenspiegel and his Nele; the Lamme Goedzak (Damme, 6 km, www.bootdamme-brugge.be; *see also page 51*), a nostalgic paddle steamer that sails between Bruges and Damme; Loppem Castle (Loppem, 6 km, www.kasteelvanloppem.be), where King Albert I resided during the liberation of Belgium at the end of the First World War; the Permeke Museum (Jabbeke, 10 km, www.muzee.be), where you can stroll around the home, garden and workshops of the renowned painter Constant Permeke; the Roman Archaeological Museum (Romeins Archeologisch Museum - RAM) (Oudenburg, 16 km, www.ram-oudenburg.be), where you can marvel at the archaeological finds from Oudenburg's glorious past; Wijnendale castle (Torhout, 23 km, www.toerismetorhout.be), a moated castle with a glorious thousand-year history, where countless rulers once resided; the Torhout Pottery Museum (Torhout, 22 km, www.toerismetorhout.be), which focuses on the rich tradition of the world-famous Torhout earthenware and is housed in the walled Ravenhof castle; and Ten Putte Abbey (Gistel, 25 km, www.godelievevangistel.be), home to the religious Moeder van Vrede (Mother of Peace) community and the place where, in particular, Saint Godelieve is honoured. There is also the well-kept Godelieve Museum, where you can learn more about the life of Gistel's very own saint.

Loppem Castle

Coast

The Coast never loses its appeal. From De Panne to Knokke-Heist, each seaside resort has its own unique atmosphere. Old-world or contemporary, picturesque or chic, intimate or urbane, the seaside towns are all purveyors of the good life. Nature galore, an abundance of culture, wonderful sandy beaches, inviting shopping streets, traffic-free promenades that are ideal for a bracing seaside stroll: this is the coast in a nutshell! And the regular tram service (www.dekusttram.be) allows you to travel from one resort to another in no time at all. Taste that salty sea air, enjoy the mild climate and treat yourself to a delicious meal with the very best the North Sea has to offer.

INFO > www.dekust.be

Not to be missed

During the Heritage Walk in Zeebrugge (shop.westoer.be) you will learn about the sea port of Bruges. The route (follow the studs in the ground) highlights the role of Zeebrugge in the Flemish fishing industry and in the First World War. Or perhaps you prefer to see the harbour from the water? The harbour tour on the passenger boat 'Zephira' (Zeebrugge, 14 km, www.franlis.be, *see also page 51*) takes you to one of the world's biggest locks. Also visit the Old Fish Market, where you can discover the rich history of the sea in the Seafront maritime theme park (Zeebrugge,

Zeebrugge

THE NEW CRUISE TERMINAL PUTS ZEEBRUGGE AT YOUR FEET

The Zeebrugge skyline has recently welcomed a remarkable addition with the completion of the brand-new cruise terminal at the Rederskaai. The seven-storey tower symbolizes a modern belfry, which highlights the historical link between the port of Zeebrugge and the city of Bruges. Cruise passengers are given a warm welcome here, but even if you are not planning to set sail you can still drop in for a visit. The top floor 'harbours' the rooftop restaurant Njord, where you can sample delicious dishes and coastal specialities while enjoying the wide panoramic view. The port, North Sea coast and even the Bruges skyline are all at your feet!

14 km, www.seafront.be, *see also page 69*). The buildings of the Old Fish Market are also home to various shops, restaurants and cafes. In the Belle Epoque Centre in Blankenberge (Blankenberge, 14 km, www.belle.epoque.blankenberge.be) you can explore this exciting transition period between the 19th and 20th centuries, a carefree world of grandeur and luxury along the Belgian coast. In Ostend, Mu.ZEE is a 'must-see' (Ostend, 22 km, www.muzee.be), with its unique collection of modern and contemporary Belgian art and a brand-new wing devoted to the work of grandmasters James Ensor, Raoul Servais and Léon Spilliaert. Ensor is also the focus in The James Ensor House (Ostend, 22 km, www.ensorstad.be), the recently renovated experience centre where, from autumn of 2019, you can step into the fascinating world of Ostend's most famous painter. If you're hungry for more culture the permanent Beaufort sculpture park (www.belgiancoast.co.uk/en/inspiration/sculpture-park-beaufort) should be right up your alley: modern masterpieces from previous editions of this art triennial are scattered throughout various coastal towns and cities. To round it all off, you can unwind amidst the magnificent fauna and flora of the Zwin Nature Park (Knokke-Heist, 20 km, www.zwin.be), 'the international bird airport'.

Knokke-Heist, Zwin Nature Park

Westhoek

Endless panoramic views, gently rolling hills, flat polders and a breath-taking silence. The landscape where the terrible battles of the Great War were once fought are now a calm and peaceful natural paradise with limitless pleasure. This green region, sandwiched between the French border and the North Sea coast, is dotted with numerous picturesque villages, where you can not only discover the sad history and the silent witnesses of the First World War, but also enjoy a bite to eat and a refreshing drink at one of the many charming restaurants and taverns, often located in the most idyllic settings. A joy for walkers and cyclists. Why not sample a Picon, the delicious borderland aperitif? One thing is certain; wherever you go and whatever you do, you will always be welcomed with the same Westhoek friendliness.
INFO > www.toerismewesthoek.be

Not to be missed

The In Flanders Fields Museum (Ypres, 46 km, www.inflandersfields.be), housed in the historic Cloth Hall in the centre of Ypres, tells in an impressively

GUIDED EXCURSIONS TO THE WESTHOEK

Make a poignant but memorable (mini-) bus tour, leaving from Bruges, through the countless reminders of the First World War in the Westhoek, with Quasimodo Tours (www.quasimodo.be), the In Flanders Fields – The Great War tour (www.brussels-citytours.be) or Flanders Fields Battlefield Daytours (www.visitbruges.org). You can also make an excursion to the Westhoek with the following (taxi) companies: Taxi Snel (www.taxisnel.be) and Poppies Day Tours (www.poppiesdaytours.be).

Langemark-Poelkapelle, *The Brooding Soldier*

Site John McCrae, Ypres

Lo-Reninge, Jules Destrooper Visitors' Centre

modern and interactive manner the tragic story of the First World War in the West Flanders front region. In the same building, you can also visit the new Yper Museum (Ypres, 46 km, www.ypermuseum.be), devoted to this historic city which somehow always seems to land on its feet. Also in Ypres is the Last Post Ceremony (Ypres, 46 km, www.lastpost.be), a daily tribute to the dead of the Great War, which takes place at 8 o'clock sharp each evening at the Menin Gate, an imposing memorial that bears the names of 54,896 British soldiers whose bodies could not be identified. In the same way, CWGC Tyne Cot Cemetery (Passendale, 54 km, www.passchendaele.be, www.cwgc.org), the largest British military cemetery in Europe, makes tangible the immense human cost of the First World War. The Memorial Museum Passchendaele 1917 (Zonnebeke, 66 km, www.passchendaele.be) relates the historical narrative of the war in a dramatic and visual manner, with special attention for the Battle of Passchendaele.

For families with children, Beauvoorde Castle (Wulveringem, 56 km, www.kasteelbeauvoorde.be) is well worth a visit. Here, you will be transported back to the romantic age of knights and their damsels, and can also enjoy one of the many family activities organized in the elegant castle park in the Anglo-French style. The Jules Destrooper Visitors' Centre (Lo-Reninge, 70 km, www.julesdestrooper.com) leads you through the rich history of this biscuit-making family and rewards you at the end of your visit with a sample tasting. Equally tasty is the Hop Museum in Poperinge (Poperinge, 83 km, www.hopmuseum.be), where you can learn everything you ever wanted to know about hops, which, you may be surprised to discover, are used for much more than just making beer!

Ypres, Last Post

Tourist office 't Zand (Concert Hall)

Bruges practical

Travelling to and in Bruges

Up-to-date information about access can be found on www.visitbruges.be

By car

From the UK you can travel to Bruges by ferry or by Eurotunnel:

» **Hull (UK) – Zeebrugge (B)** with P&O Ferries (crossing: 1 night). Take the N31 from Zeebrugge to Bruges. Estimated distance Zeebrugge – Bruges is 17 km or 11 miles (30 min driving).

» **Dover (UK) – Dunkerque (F)** with DFDS Seaways (crossing: 2h00). Take the motorway E40 to Bruges. Estimated distance Dunkerque – Bruges is 76 km or 47 miles (1h driving).

» **Dover (UK) – Calais (F)** with P&O Ferries or DFDS Seaways (crossing: 1h30). Estimated distance Calais – Bruges is 120 km or 75 miles (1h30 driving).

» **Folkestone (UK) – Calais (F)** via Eurotunnel (35 min). Estimated distance Calais – Bruges is 120 km or 75 miles (1h30 driving).

A 30 kph zone is in force throughout the entire city centre. This means that you are forbidden at all times to drive faster than 30 kilometres per hour. Parking is for an unlimited time and is most advantageous in one of the two city centre car parks. *(For more information, see 'Parking'.)*

P Parking

Bruges is a compact city, made for people. The use of motorized transport in the historic city centre is discouraged. There are a number of outlying car parks within easy walking distance of the centre where you can park **free of charge**. A little further away are the park&ride cark parks, also free, from which you can reach the centre by bike or public transport. A blue zone has been created around the city centre. You can park free of charge for a limited period in this blue zone (max. 4 hours) between 9.00 a.m. and 6.00 p.m. Always remember to use your parking disc! Between 9.00 a.m. and 8.00 p.m. above ground parking in the city centre is limited in time (min. 30 min. and max. 4 hours) and metered, also on Sundays and public holidays (1st hour: €1.80; 2nd, 3rd and 4th hours: €2.40; max. €9 for 4 hours). Payment can be made via an SMS/text message, using the 4411 app (only for Belgian mobile phone numbers) or by cash or bank card at one of the parking ticket machines. The correct number plate of your car must always be entered into the machine. Parking in the city centre for an unlimited period is **cheapest** in the public cark parks in front of the railway station (City Map: D13) and under the 't Zand square. Both car parks are within easy walking distance of the market square, or else you can use one of the city buses operated by De Lijn *(for more info, see the section on 'Public transport')*. The bus transfer (max. 4 people per car) from the Centrum-Station car park to the city centre and back is included in the price of the parking ticket. If you are staying overnight in Bruges, ask your hotel or guesthouse about parking options in the vicinity.

INFO > You can find the most up-to-date parking information on www.visitbruges.be

▸ Parking Centrum-Station

Stationsplein | City map: D13

CAPACITY > 1500

OPEN > Daily, 24 hours a day

PRICE > Maximum €3.50/24 hrs | hourly rate: €0.70 | including free bus transfer (max. 4 people per car)

▸ Parking Centrum-'t Zand

Underneath 't Zand | City map: C9
CAPACITY > 1400
OPEN > Daily, 24 hours a day
PRICE > Maximum €8.70/24 hrs | hourly rate: €1.20; from the second hour you pay per quarter hour

By bus

Several international coach companies organize connections to Bruges from important international transport hubs and foreign cities. The bus stops for these services are on the Sint-Michiels' side (Spoorwegstraat) of the main railway station. There is also a Flixbus stop on the Bargeplein.

▸ To and from transport hubs

From Brussels South Charleroi Airport **flibco.com** runs several direct services each day. **Ouibus** organizes direct services from and to Lille-Europe HST station on a daily basis. The journey times are arranged to match the times of the Eurostar trains and the TGV. **Flixbus** has connections to and from several international transport hubs; namely, the TGV/HST stations at Brussel-Zuid (Brussels South) and Lille-Europe, as well as the airports at Frankfurt (terminal 2), Cologne, Brussels (Zaventem), Amsterdam (Schiphol) and Paris (both Charles de Gaulle and Orly).

▸ To and from foreign cities

Flixbus, **Ouibus** and **Eurolines** organize regular services to and from Bruges. The buses stop in various Belgian, Dutch, French, German, English and Czech cities. It is recommended to always book your seat in advance (for some companies it is obligatory). See www.ouibus.com, www.flixbus.com and www.eurolines.eu for up-to-date information about arrival/departure times, fare prices and reservations.

By train

▸ National

Every day, there are from one to four direct services each hour between Bruges and the important train junctions at Antwerp, Ghent, Hasselt, Leuven and Brussels. Please consult www.belgiantrain.be.

▸ International

The Brussels-South Station (Brussel-Zuid/-Midi) is the Belgian hub for international rail traffic (www.b-europe.com). Numerous high-speed trains arrive in Brussel-Zuid daily, coming from Paris (Thalys/Izy and TGV), Lille (Eurostar, TGV and Thalys), London (Eurostar), Amsterdam (NS InterCity, Thalys and Eurostar) and Cologne (Thalys and ICE). Every day, there are three trains an hour from Brussels-South Station, which stop at Bruges on their way to Ostend, Knokke or Blankenberge. The travelling time between Brussel-South and Bruges is approximately 1 hour.

By plane

▸ Via Brussels Airport-Zaventem

The national airport daily receives flights from more than 200 cities in 85 countries. It is easy to travel from Brussels Airport-Zaventem to Bruges by train. Every day there is a direct hourly service to Bruges. In addition, many other trains from Brussels Airport-Zaventem regularly stop at Brussels-North, Brussels-Central or Brussels-South railway stations. From these three stations there are three trains an hour daily stopping at Bruges on their way to Ostend, Knokke or Blankenberge. Consult www.belgiantrain.be for information about arrival-departure times and fare prices. For those who prefer to take a taxi, you can find all the relevant information on page 153.

▸ Via Brussels South Charleroi Airport

This popular regional airport receives multiple low-cost flights every day from various cities and regions in and outside of Europe. The flibco.com bus company (www.flibco.com) provides several direct shuttle bus services to and from the station in Bruges on a daily basis. For those who prefer to take a taxi, you can find all the relevant information on page 153.

▸ Via Ostend-Bruges Airport

The Ostend-Bruges Airport is in full development and systematically expands its offer. The railway station at Ostend is just a 15-minute bus ride away. From here, there are at least three trains to Bruges each hour between 6.00 a.m. and 10.00 p.m., with final destinations in Eupen, Welkenraedt, Brussels Airport-Zaventem, Antwerpen-Centraal or Kortrijk. The train journey to Bruges takes about 15 minutes. Consult www.belgiantrain.be for information about arrival-departure times and fare prices. For those who prefer to take a taxi, you can find all the relevant information on page 153.

Public transport

You can find the most up-to-date travel information on www.visitbruges.be

▸ Bus

Public transport in Bruges is well organised. Buses run every three minutes between the station and the city centre. There are also frequent services to the train station and the city centre running from the bus stop for tourist buses at the Kanaaleiland ('canal Island'; City map: E13). The buses going to the city centre stop within easy walking distance of the main shopping streets, historical buildings and museums. The most important bus stops are marked on the city map (see the folding map on the inside of the back cover).
A ticket allows you to change bus services as many times as you want for a period of 60 minutes. The ticket price is €3. All De Lijn tickets can be bought at the following points of sale.

How to get to Bruges?

departure	via	km	miles	time boat	time train	time bus	make a reservation
Amsterdam	Brussels-South/Midi	253	157	-	± 3:10	-	www.thalys.com, www.eurostar.com www.nsinternational.nl
Brussels Airport-Zaventem	-	110	68	-	± 1:30	-	www.belgiantrain.be
Brussels South Charleroi Airport	-	148	92	-	-	2:10	www.flibco.com
Ostend-Bruges Airport	Oostende	24	15	-	*see above*		www.delijn.be, www.belgiantrain.be
Dover	Dunkerque	-	-	2:00	-	-	www.dfdsseaways.com
Dover	Calais	-	-	1:30	-	-	www.poferries.com, www.dfdsseaways.com
Hull	Zeebrugge	-	-	1 night	-		www.poferries.com
Lille Flandres	Kortrijk	75	47	-	± 1:47	-	www.b-europe.com
London St Pancras	Brussels-South/Midi	-	-	-	± 3:25	-	www.eurostar.com

▸ Tickets

» Advance sales offices

- De Lijnwinkel, Stationsplein
- Tourist office on ℹ 't Zand (Concert Hall)
- Various book stores, newsagents and supermarkets in the city centre

» Vending machines De Lijn

- De Lijnwinkel, Stationsplein
- Bus stop 't Zand

Taxis

TAXI STANDS

- At Bruges station: city centre side and Sint-Michiels side
- At the Bargeweg (Kanaaleiland)
- On the Markt
- In the Vlamingstraat (opposite the City Theatre)
- In the Boeveriestraat (near 't Zand)
- In the Kuipersstraat (next to the library)

PRICE > The local taxi companies all use the same fixed-rate tariffs (adjustments are possible throughout the year):

- Bruges <> Brussels Airport-Zaventem: €200
- Bruges <> Brussels South Charleroi Airport: €250
- Bruges <> Aéroport de Lille/ train stations in Lille: €140
- Bruges <> Ostend-Bruges Airport: €70
- Bruges <> Brussels (city centre): €175
- Bruges (railway station, Bargeplein or Boeveriestraat) <> Zeebrugge cruisterminal: €55

You can find a list of licensed taxi companies and their contact details on www.visitbruges.be

Bike taxi

BIKE TAXI STANDS

- Markt (near the Historium)
- 't Zand (near the Concert Hall)
- Stationsplein (Kiss&Ride)

PRICE > Rates can be obtained (on-site) from the individual bike taxi companies.
INFO > Tel. +32 (0)471 04 86 07 or www.taxifietsbrugge.be, tel. +32 (0)478 40 95 57 or www.fietskoetsenbrugge.be and tel. +32 (0)478 51 41 15 or www.greenrides.eu

In Bruges

From the station in Bruges, you can travel every three minutes to your overnight accommodation address by De Lijn bus *(see 'Public transport')* or by taxi *(see 'Taxis')*.

Practical information

Accessibility

Various locations in Bruges have facilities for people with a disability. They are indicated in this guide with , , and . These icons will allow you to easily recognize the locations that have facilities for people with physical, mental, visual, and/or hearing impairments. You can find more details about the level of accessibility in the tourist offices. There you can also pick up a copy of a free folder (Dutch or English), which includes an easily accessible walking route that will take you past the most important sites of interest. Along the route you can find plenty of accessible accommodation, catering outlets and public toilets. The folder also contains lots of other useful practical tips.

Bicycle rental

» **Bauhaus Bike Rental**
LOCATION > Langestraat 145
PRICE > 3 hours: €6; full day: €10
OPEN > 1/3 to 30/9: daily, 8.00 a.m.-8.00 p.m.; 1/10 to 28/2: daily, 8.00 a.m.-5.00 p.m.
INFO > Tel. +32 (0)50 34 10 93, www.bauhaus.be

» **B-Bike Concertgebouw**
LOCATION > Concert Hall, 't Zand
PRICE > 1 hour: €4; 5 hours: €10; full day: €12. Tandem, full day: €22. Electric bike, full day: €22
OPEN > 1/3 to 31/10: daily, 10.00 a.m.-7.00 p.m.; 1/11 to 28/2: open by appointment only. Bicycles can be returned until 10.00 p.m.
INFO > Tel. +32 (0)50 61 26 67 or +32 (0)479 97 12 80, www.bensbike.be

» **Bruges Bike Rental**
LOCATION > Niklaas Desparsstraat 17
PRICE > 1 hour: €4; 2 hours: €7; 4 hours: €10; full day: €13, students (on display of a valid student card): €10. Electric bike, 1 hour: €10; 2 hours: €15; 4 hours: €22, full day: €30. Tandem, 1 hour: €10; 2 hours: €15; 4 hours: €20; full day: €25, students (on display of a valid student card): €22
OPEN > Daily, 10.00 a.m.-8.00 p.m.
ADDITIONAL CLOSING DATES > 1/1 and 25/12
INFO > Tel. +32 (0)50 61 61 08, www.brugesbikerental.be

» **De Ketting**
LOCATION > Gentpoortstraat 23
PRICE > Full day: €8. Electric bike, full day: €22
OPEN > Tuesday to Saturday, 10.00 a.m.-6.00 p.m.; Monday and Sunday, 10.30 a.m.-6.00 p.m.
ADDITIONAL CLOSING DATES > Sundays during the period 16/10 to 31/3
INFO > Tel. +32 (0)50 34 41 96, www.deketting.be

» **Fietsen Popelier**
LOCATION > Mariastraat 26
PRICE > 1 hour: €5; 4 hours: €10; full day: €15. Electric bike or tandem, 1 hour: €10; 4 hours: €20; full day: €30
OPEN > 15/3 to 31/10: daily, 9.00 a.m.-7.00 p.m.; 1/11 to 14/3: daily, 10.00 a.m.-6.00 p.m.
ADDITIONAL CLOSING DATES > 1/1, 30/5 and 25/12; closed on Monday in January and December
INFO > Tel. +32 (0)50 34 32 62, www.fietsenpopelier.be

» **Fietspunt Station**
LOCATION > Hendrik Brugmansstraat 3 (Stationsplein)

PRICE > 1 hour: €6; 4 hours: €10; full day: €15. Electric bike, 4 hours: €20; full day: €30
OPEN > Monday to Friday, 7.00 a.m.-7.00 p.m.; 1/5 to 30/9: also during weekends and public holidays, 9.00 a.m.-5.00 p.m.
ADDITIONAL CLOSING DATES > 25/12 to 1/1
INFO > Tel. +32 (0)50 39 68 26, www.fietspunten.be

» Koffieboontje
LOCATION > Hallestraat 4
PRICE > 1 hour: €5; 5 hours: €10; full day: €15, students (on display of a valid student card): €11.25. Tandem, 1 hour: €10; 5 hours: €20; full day: €30, students (on display of a valid student card): €22.50
OPEN > Daily, 9.00 a.m.-10.00 p.m
EXTRA > Wheelchair and pushchair rental
INFO > Tel. +32 (0)50 33 80 27, www.bikerentalkoffieboontje.be

» La Bicicleta
LOCATION > Wijngaardstraat 13
PRICE > Full day: €15
OPEN > Daily, 11.00 a.m.-10.00 p.m., book in advance via the website.
INFO > Tel. +32 (0)478 33 49 69, www.labicicleta.be

» Snuffel Hostel
LOCATION > Ezelstraat 42
PRICE > Full day: €8
OPEN > Daily, 8.00 a.m.-8.00 p.m.
INFO > Tel. +32 (0)50 33 31 33, www.snuffel.be

» Steershop
LOCATION > Koolkerkse Steenweg 7a
Hired bicycles can be delivered to the address of your accommodation.
PRICE > Full day: €15
OPEN > Tuesday to Saturday, 8.00 a.m.-11.00 a.m. and 4.00 p.m.-8.00 p.m. (Saturday until 6.00 p.m.)
EXTRA > Guided tours *(see page 142)*
INFO > Tel. +32 (0)474 40 84 01, www.steershop.be

Most of the bicycle rental points ask for the payment of a guarantee.

Campers

The Kanaaleiland ('Canal Island') at the Bargeweg offers an excellent camping site for at least 40 camping cars all year round. Once your camper is parked, you are just a five-minute walk from the city centre (via the Beguinage). It is not possible to make prior reservations.
PRICE > 1/4 to 30/9: €25/day; 1/10 to 31/3: €19/day. Free electricity; it is also possible to stock up on free clean water (€0.50) and dispose of dirty water.
OPEN > You can enter the site between 8.00 a.m. and 10.00 p.m. You can leave at any time.
INFO > www.interparking.com

Church services

01 Basiliek van het Heilig Bloed (Basilica of the Holy Blood)
Daily, except Mondays: 11.00 a.m.

02 Begijnhofkerk (Beguinage Church)
Monday to Saturday: 11.00 a.m., Sunday and public holidays: 9.30 a.m.

04 English Convent
Monday to Saturday: 7.45 a.m.

12 English Church
('t Keerske / Saint Peter's Chapel)
English language Anglican service, Sunday: 6.00 p.m. (27/10 to 24/3: 5.00 p.m.)

10 Kapucijnenkerk (Capuchins Church)
Monday to Friday: 8.00 a.m. (Tuesday: also 6.00 p.m.), Saturday: 6.00 p.m., Sunday: 10.00 a.m.

11 Karmelietenkerk (Carmelites Church)
Monday to Friday: 12.00 p.m., Sunday: 10.00 a.m.

15 Onze-Lieve-Vrouwekerk (Church of Our Lady)
Saturday: 5.30 p.m., Sunday: 11.00 a.m.

16 Onze-Lieve-Vrouw-ter-Potteriekerk (Church of Our Lady of the Pottery)
Sunday: 7.00 a.m. and 9.30 a.m.

17 Onze-Lieve-Vrouw-van-Blindekens-kapel (Chapel of Our Lady of the Blind)
First Saturday of the month: 6.00 p.m.

18 Orthodoxe Kerk HH. Konstantijn & Helena (Orthodox Church Saints Constantin & Helen)
Saturday: 6.00 p.m., Sunday: 9.00 a.m.

19 Sint-Annakerk (Saint Anne's Church)
Sunday: 9.00 a.m.

20 Sint-Gilliskerk (Saint Giles' Church)
Sunday: 7.00 p.m.

22 Sint-Jakobskerk (Saint James's Church)
Wednesday and Saturday: 7.00 p.m.

23 Sint-Salvatorskathedraal (Saint Saviour's Cathedral)
Monday to Friday: 6.00 p.m. (Friday: also 8.30 a.m.), Saturday: 4.00 p.m., Sunday: 10.30 a.m.

12 Verenigde Protestantse Kerk (United Protestant Church)
('t Keerske / Saint Peter's Chapel)
Sunday: 10.00 a.m.

25 Vrije Evangelische Kerk (Free Evangelical Church)
Sunday: 10.00 a.m.

Cinemas

All films are shown in their original language. Subtitles in Dutch and/or French are added when necessary.

15 Cinema Lumière
Sint-Jakobsstraat 36, tel. +32 (0)50 34 34 65, www.lumierecinema.be

16 Kinepolis Brugge
Koning Albert I-laan 200, Sint-Michiels, tel. +32 (0)50 30 50 00, www.kinepolis.com | scheduled bus no. 27, bus stop: Kinepolis

Discount cards and combi-tickets

You can get discounts for your visits to various museums, sites of interest and attractions in Bruges if you use a discount card or combiticket. *You can find more info on page 75.*

Emergencies

▸ European emergency number: tel. 112

This free general number is used in all the member states of the European Union to call for assistance from the police, fire brigade or ambulance service: daily, 24 hours a day.

▸ Medical help

» Doctors, pharmacists, dentists and nursing officers on duty
Tel. 1733. For non-urgent medical help during the evening, night and at weekends.

» Hospitals

- A.Z. St.-Jan > tel. +32 (0)50 45 21 11
- A.Z. St.-Lucas > tel. +32 (0)50 36 91 11
- St.-Franciscus Xaveriuskliniek > tel. +32 (0)50 47 04 70

» Poisons Advice Centre
tel. +32 (0)70 245 245

Formalities

» Identity
An identity card or valid passport is necessary. An ordinary identity card is sufficient for most citizens of the European Union. If you arrive in Belgium from outside the European Union, you must first pass through customs. There are no border controls once

inside the European Union. Check at the Belgian embassy or at the consulate in your home country in advance to find out exactly what documents you need.

» **Health**

Citizens of the European Union have access to unanticipated, urgent medical care in Belgium through their own national health insurance card/document. This care is given under the same conditions as for the local Belgian population and assures full or partial reimbursement of the medical costs. You can obtain this card from your own national health service. Please note, however, that every member of the family must have his/her own card/document.

Good to know

Don't let pickpockets ruin your shopping trip. Always keep your **wallet/purse** in a closed inside pocket, and not in an open handbag or rucksack. A golden tip for ladies: always close your handbag and wear it with the fastener against your body. Bruges is a lively, fun-loving city with great nightlife. Please bear in mind that it is prohibited to sell, give or serve **spirits** (whisky, gin, rum, vodka, etc.) to people under the age of 18 years. For people under the age of 16, this prohibition applies for all drinks with an alcohol content exceeding 0.5%. When purchasing alcohol, proof of age may be requested. All drugs – including cannabis – are prohibited by law in Belgium. Visiting Bruges means endless hours of fun, but please allow the visitors who come after you to enjoy their stay in a **clean** and **tidy** city: so always put your rubbish in a rubbish bin.

Inhabitants

On 1 January 2018, there were 19,574 inhabitants registered as living in the inner city of Bruges. The total population of Greater Bruges on the same date was 117,915.

Lockers

» **Station (railway station)**

Stationsplein | City map: C13

» 26 **Historium**

Markt 1

Market days

» **Mondays**

8.00 a.m.-1.30 p.m. | Onder de Toren – Lissewege | miscellaneous

» **Wednesdays**

8.00 a.m.-1.30 p.m. | Markt | food and flowers

» **Fridays**

8.00 a.m.-1.30 p.m. | Market Square – Zeebrugge | miscellaneous

» **Saturdays**

8.00 a.m.-1.30 p.m. | 't Zand | miscellaneous

» **Sundays**

7.00 a.m.-2.00 p.m. | Veemarkt, Sint-Michiels | miscellaneous

» **Wednesday to Saturday**

8.00 a.m.-1.30 p.m. | Vismarkt | fish

» **Daily**

During the period 15/3 to 15/11: 9.00 a.m.-5.00 p.m.; during the period 16/11 to 14/3: 10.00 a.m.-4.00 p.m. | Vismarkt | artisanal products

» **Saturdays, Sundays, public holidays and bridge days in the period 15/3 to 15/11 + also on Fridays in the period June to September**

10.00 a.m.-6.00 p.m. | Dijver | antique, bric-à-brac and crafts

Money

Most of the banks in Bruges are open from 9.00 a.m. to 12.30 p.m. and from 2.00 p.m. to 4.30 p.m. Some branch offices are also open on Saturday morning, but on Sundays they are all closed. There are cash points in several shopping streets, on 't Zand, Simon Stevinplein and Stationsplein. You can easily withdraw money from cash machines with Visa, Eurocard or MasterCard. You can exchange money in one of the currency exchange offices. In the event of the loss or theft of your bank or credit card, it is best to immediately block the card by calling Card Stop on tel. 070 344 344 (24 hours a day).

» **Exchange office Western Union**
INFO > Steenstraat 2, tel. +32 (0)50 34 04 71

» **Exchange office Pillen bvba**
INFO > Vlamingstraat 18, tel. +32 (0)50 44 20 55

» **Exchange office Moneytrans Brugge**
INFO > Rozenhoedkaai 2, tel. +32 (0)50 34 59 55

Opening hours

Cafés and restaurants have no (fixed) closing hour. Sometimes they will remain open until the early hours of the morning and other days they will close earlier: it all depends on the number of customers.
(See 'Shopping in Bruges' for info about shop opening times, page 88.)

Police

» **General telephone number**
tel. +32 (0)50 44 88 44

» **Emergency police assistance** tel. 101

» **Central district**
Monday to Friday: 8.00 a.m.-5.00 p.m. and Saturdays: 9.00 a.m.-6.00 p.m. | Kartuizerinnenstraat 4 | City map: E9

» **Police Station**
Monday to Thursday: 7.00 a.m.- 9.00 p.m. and continuously from 7.00 a.m. on Friday to 9.00 p.m. on Sunday. For urgent matters, there is a permanent 24-hour service in the police station | Lodewijk Coiseaukaai 3 | City map: F1

Post office

Smedenstraat 57-59 | City map: B9
You can also make use of one of the post points (advice, dispatch, stamps, etc.); stamps can also be bought in one of the various stamp outlets in the shopping streets or from the i tourist office on 't Zand (Concert Hall).

Public holidays

On public holidays most companies, shops, offices and public services are closed.

> 1 January (New Year's Day)
> 21 April (Easter Sunday) and 22 April (Easter Monday)
> 1 May (Labour Day)
> 30 May (Ascension Day)
> 9 June (Whit Sunday) and 10 June (Whit Monday)
> 11 July (Flemish regional holiday)
> 21 July (Belgian national holiday)
> 15 August (Assumption of Mary)
> 1 November (All Saints' Day)
> 11 November (Armistice Day)
> 25 December (Christmas)
> 26 December (Boxing Day)

Scooter rental

Vespa Tours
LOCATION > Estaminet 't Molenhuis, Potterierei 109
PRICE PER VESPA > Including helmet and insurance, 5 hours: €50 (1 person) or €65 (2 people); full day: €70 (1 person) or €80 (2 people)
OPEN > 1/3 to 31/10: daily, 10.00 a.m.-6.00 p.m.
CONDITIONS > Minimum age of driver: 21 years, driver's license B
INFO > Tel. +32 (0)497 64 86 48

Smoking

In Belgium there is a general ban on smoking in cafés, restaurants, public areas in hotels (lobby, bar, corridors, etc.) and in all public buildings (train stations, airports, etc.). Those unable to kick the habit will usually find an ashtray just outside.

Swimming pools

11 Interbad

Six 25-meter lanes; also a recreational pool, water slide, toddler's pool and teaching pool.

INFO > Veltemweg 35, Sint-Kruis, tel. +32 (0)50 35 07 77, interbad@skynet.be, www.interbad.be; scheduled bus no. 10, no. 58 or no. 58S, bus stop: Watertoren

12 Jan Guilini

25-meter indoor pool in a beautiful listed building, named after the swimming champion and resistance fighter Jan Guilini.

INFO > Keizer Karelstraat 41, tel. +32 (0)50 31 35 54, zwembadjanguilini@brugge.be, www.brugge.be/sport; scheduled bus no. 9, bus stop: Visartpark

13 Lago Brugge Olympia

An Olympic size pool (50 metres), a 'subtropical swimming paradise' (including slides, a wave pool, a wild-water run), an outdoor sunbathing area (with two outdoor pools and several attractions) and various wellness facilities.

INFO > Doornstraat 110, Sint-Andries, tel. +32 (0)50 67 28 70, olympia@lago.be, www.lago.be/brugge; scheduled bus no. 5, bus stop: Lange Molen or no. 25, bus stop: Jan Breydel

All information about opening times is available at the i tourist office Markt (Historium), 't Zand (Concert Hall) or Stationsplein (railway station).

Telephones

If you want to phone someone in Bruges from abroad, you must first dial the country code (00)32, followed by the zone code 50, and the number of the person you want to contact. To phone Bruges from within Belgium, you dial 050 plus the number of the person.

Toilets

There are a number of public toilets in Bruges (see WC on the fold-out plan at the back of the guide). When local people need to use a toilet, they often pop into a cafe or pub to order something small so that they can use the facilities there.

Tourist offices

» **Tourist office Markt (Historium)**
Daily, 10.00 a.m.-5.00 p.m.

» **Tourist office 't Zand (Concert Hall)**
Monday to Saturday, 10.00 a.m.-5.00 p.m.; Sundays and public holidays, 10.00 a.m.-2.00 p.m.

» **Tourist office Railway Station (corridor to the platforms, city centre side)**
Daily, 10.00 a.m.-5.00 p.m.

All tourist offices are closed on Christmas Day and New Year's Day. Tel. +32 (0)50 44 46 46, visitbruges@brugge.be, www.visitbruges.be

Travelling season and climate

Although most visitors come to the city in the spring and summer months, Bruges has something to offer all year round. The misty months of autumn and winter are ideal for atmospheric strolls along the canals and the cobbled streets, before ending up in a cosy restaurant or cheerful pub. Ambiance guaranteed, although every now and then you may have to put up with a little rain, so make sure you bring an umbrella! The 'cold' months are also perfect for undisturbed visits to the city's many museums and sites of interest, before again finishing up in one of those same restaurants or pubs! What's more, in January, February, March and often on weekdays as well, you can get great discounts on many accommodation outlets in Bruges.

Index of street names